Women, men and language

Studies in language and linguistics

General editors: G. N. Leech & M. H. Short,
University of Lancaster

Already published:

Women, men and language
   Jennifer Coates

CU

Women, men and language
A sociolinguistic account of sex differences in language

Jennifer Coates

Longman
London & New York

Longman Group UK Limited
Longman House, Burnt Mill. Harlow
Essex CM20 2JE, England
Associated companies throughout the world

*Published in the United States of America
by Longman Inc., New York*

First published 1986

British Library Cataloguing in Publication Data
Coates, Jennifer
  Women, men and language: a sociolinguistic
  account of sex differences in language. —
  (Studies in language and linguistics)
  1. Language and languages — Sex differences
  I. Title   II. Series
  418   P120.S48
  ISBN 0-582-29133-X

Library of Congress Cataloging in Publication Data
Coates, Jennifer.
  Women, men and language.

  (Studies in language and linguistics)
  Bibliography: p.
  Includes index.
  1. Language and languages — Sex differences. I. Title.
II. Series.
P25.S7 [P120.S48]   401'.9   85-23716
ISBN 0-582-29133-X

Set in Linotron 202 10/11 pt Times
Produced by Longman Group (FE) Limited
Printed in Hong Kong

Contents

Preface

Sex differences are a topic of perennial interest in our society, but it is not generally understood that most sex differences are the result of social, not biological, pressures, and moreover our 'common-sense' understanding of such differences is heavily influenced by the cultural myths we have all absorbed. In this book, I have tried to improve our understanding in both these areas. I discuss the way women and men are socialised into differing gender roles, and show how the linguistic usage of women and men reflects these differences. I have also tried to lay bare the myths about linguistic sex differences current in our culture (I call this folklinguistics), and have described research which attempts to show how women and men actually *do* talk. One of the most interesting findings to emerge is that, in a general way, it is possible to talk of 'women's style' and 'men's style'. Particularly in the context of single-sex groups, women and men talk in very different ways: this has led some researchers to describe the conversation typical of all-women's groups as 'co-operative' and that typical of all-men's groups as 'competitive'. It is surely desirable that, as speakers, we all have access to as wide a range of styles as possible. The ideal, androgynous speaker would be able to switch from assertiveness to tentativeness as circumstances required, and would be as good at *listening* as at speaking.

' Clearly women and men could learn from each other's styles; this would benefit not only the individual speaker, but would also cut down miscommunication in mixed groups. However, these are pious hopes. Linguistic differences are merely a reflection of social differences, and as long as society views women and men as different – and unequal – then differences in the language of women and men will persist.

London, January 1986.   **J.C.**

vi

Acknowledgements

This book arose from a course I taught for many years at Edge Hill College. I am grateful to Stanley Ellis and Mark Newbrook for providing me with information about their work, and to Chris Baldick, Rhiannon Evans, Sarah Kay and Edward Wilson for their suggestions of folklinguistic material. I have been enormously helped by those who read and commented on earlier drafts of parts of the book: Deborah Cameron, Jenny Cheshire, Margaret Deuchar, Dick Leith, Beryl Madoc-Jones, Lesley Milroy. I would also like to thank my editors, Geoff Leech and Mick Short, for their comments and advice on the manuscript. But my main thanks are reserved for Joy Bowes whose scrupulously careful and detailed comments and criticisms on every chapter of the book have been invaluable. The book is dedicated to the students who took my course – it was their interest in the topic and their frustration with the paucity of texts which stimulated me to write it.

Part One
Introductory

Chapter One

Language and sex

1.1   INTRODUCTION

Do women and men talk differently? This book is an attempt to
answer the question. We shall look at evidence from anthropology, dialectology, sociolinguistics and social psychology,
firstly to establish that the language of women and men *does* differ,
and secondly to show *how* it differs. We shall also attempt to
answer the question that inevitably follows: *Why* do women and
men talk differently?

There is now considerable interest in the sociolinguistic
variation associated with speaker's sex. However, the few books in
the field are mostly written from an American standpoint and for a
general audience. Articles on the subject are scattered in learned
journals, and are not always easily obtainable. In addition, details
which improve our knowledge of sex differentiation in language
occur in many sociolinguistic studies whose stated aim is to analyse
social class stratification or the speech of ethnic minorities. It is
one of the aims of this book to provide a coherent account of such
work; to bring together the many accounts of sex differences in
language that have been written and to make them accessible to
the interested reader. The book is intended both for those with an
interest in sociolinguistics who want to study one aspect of
variation in depth, and also for those interested in sex differences
in general. It will concentrate on sociolinguistic work carried out in
Britain and throughout will focus primarily on the English
language.

This book, then, is primarily a sociolinguistic account of the
co-variation of language and sex. It is not about the relationship
between language and sexism, except in a very general sense; that
is, it is not about language which denigrates, or is believed to

3

denigrate, women. It will describe language *use*, in particular the differing usage of women and men as speakers.

Note that I intend to use the term **sex**, not **gender**, in this account. 'Gender' is the more accurate term: 'sex' refers to a biological distinction, while 'gender' is the term used to describe socially constructed categories based on sex – most societies operate in terms of two genders, *male* and *female*. However, 'gender' has the disadvantage that it is already a technical term in linguistics. The grammatical category of gender is used in linguistics to refer to word classes where contrasts such as masculine – feminine – neuter, animate – inanimate, etc. are found. In French, for example, the form of the article alters depending on the *gender* of the noun – *la table* (the table — feminine) but *le livre* (the book — masculine). Strictly speaking, then, this book is about the co-variation of language and gender, but in order to avoid ambiguity, the term 'sex' will be used throughout (a practice which has been adopted in most sociolinguistic writing).[1]

In this introductory chapter, we shall begin with a brief outline of sociolinguistics, since subsequent discussion of the language of women and men will be presented in sociolinguistic terms. This outline will be followed by a discussion of women as a social group. There has been a tendency in analysis of social variation (both linguistic and non-linguistic) to fail to differentiate between women and men. If we want to explore the ways in which women's and men's language differs, then it is obviously crucial that we have some idea of how women as a group differ from men as a group. In the final section of the chapter, I shall describe the two main approaches adopted by linguists to the question of sex differences in language, which differ precisely because of disagreement about the status of women as a group.

1.2 SOCIOLINGUISTICS

Sociolinguistics has been defined as the study of language in its social context. The study of language in its social context means crucially the study of **linguistic variation**. In different social contexts an individual will speak in different ways – this is called **stylistic variation**. Moreover, speakers who differ from each other in terms of age, sex, social class, ethnic group, for example, will also differ from each other in their speech, even in the same context – this is called **social variation**. Sociolinguists are interested in both stylistic and social variation.

Sociolinguists analyse speech in order to show that linguistic variation does not occur randomly but is structured: the aim of sociolinguistics is to expose the orderly heterogeneity of the normal speech community. Unlike theoretically inclined linguists, who concentrate on the imaginary sentences of the ideal speaker-hearer in a homogeneous speech community, sociolinguists choose to grapple with the utterances of real speakers in real (heterogeneous) speech communities.

Sociolinguists are principally interested in the **vernacular**, that is, speech used spontaneously among people who know each other well. They have devised all sorts of ways of getting at the vernacular, ranging from the rapid and anonymous survey to long-term participant observation. In a rapid and anonymous survey, the researcher in the guise of, for example, a shopper, asks a question or questions designed to elicit a response of sociolinguistic interest, and then discreetly notes the response in a notebook. In a study involving long-term participant observation, the researcher interacts with a group of informants over a long period of time, becoming so familiar to them that the presence of the tape-recorder is ignored. Even when using the standard interview, sociolinguists have structured it to elicit both formal and less formal styles by, for example, asking informants to recount a story about something that happened to them: the use of personal narrative tends to reduce self-consciousness in speech. This methodological inventiveness has been stimulated by socio-linguists' sensitivity to the Observer's Paradox – which is the problem faced by researchers who want to observe how people behave when they are not being observed.

Sociolinguists have borrowed the sampling techniques of sciences like botany and zoology, as have other social sciences. Informants have been selected at random from sources such as the electoral roll, and samples have reflected the composition of the community in terms of age, social class, sex, etc. (More recent sociolinguistic work has focused on the peer group; here selection of informants is not random, but can be justified in terms of the objectives of such studies.) The best sociolinguistic analyses have shown how linguistic forms vary systematically with aspects of social context such as the social class of the speaker.

Sociolinguists' interest in the vernacular reflects their conviction that the study of language should be the study of the speech of all members of the community, not the study of the dialect spoken by the privileged few. Sociolinguists regard Standard English as just another variety of English, no more and no less interesting than any other variety. Linguists, unlike sociolinguists, start from the premise that Standard English *is* English (it happens, coincidentally, to be the variety spoken by most linguists). Sociolinguists challenge this **majority** view. Not only do they pay equal attention to all varieties, but they also draw attention to the fact that non-standard varieties have their own regular phonology, morphology, syntax and lexis. The sociolinguistic approach, then, is a **minority** approach.

The terms 'majority' and 'minority' are used here to refer to differential access to power and control. A majority community is one which has power and control and majority languages or dialects are those used by majority communities. 'Minority' is a relative term. Minority communities and minority languages are defined as such by their relation to the majority community and language. The term bears no relation to number of speakers – there may be more speakers of minority languages or dialects, but these languages/dialects do not have the same status as majority languages/dialects. By extension, mainstream (Chomskyan) linguistics can be termed the majority approach to language because it concentrates on the language variety of the majority group (the powerful), while sociolinguistics can be termed the minority approach because it focuses attention on the speech of minority communities. (For further discussion of these two approaches see Deuchar & Martin-Jones 1982.)

1.2.1 Sociolinguistics and women

Why is it only recently that sociolinguists have begun to pay much attention to the co-variation of language and sex? I should like to suggest two reasons, which stem from sociolinguistics' antecedents in dialectology and linguistics.

First, although sociolinguists rejected the biased selection of informants typical of traditional dialectology, this rejection consisted initially of choosing urban rather than rural and younger as well as older informants. While many studies included informants of both sexes, studies of male speakers only continued to be carried out (e.g. Labov's study of black adolescents in Harlem (Labov 1972b); Reid's study of Edinburgh schoolboys (Reid 1976)). I know of no sociolinguistic study which has concentrated only on *female* speakers.

Second, with the reaction against mainstream linguistics came the shift in emphasis from standard to non-standard varieties which has resulted in the minority approach described above. All sorts of minority groups have come under scrutiny, in particular working-class groups, ethnic groups, adolescents. Women, however, were not perceived as a minority group. Linguistic variation co-extensive with social class, ethnicity or age was what appeared salient to early sociolinguists. As we shall see in Chapter 4, most early sociolinguistic work concentrated on the social stratification of speech. Other kinds of variation received less attention. It has taken the development of the social sciences and the growth of the women's movement to focus attention on women as a group in their own right.

1.3   WOMEN AS A SOCIAL GROUP

Women constitute a very unusual social group. For the sake of comparison, let's look at some 'normal' groups. Let's take working-class people in Belfast, West Indians in Britain, or adolescents in Reading – social groups which are reasonably easy to identify, and which have been the subject of sociolinguistic analysis (cf. Milroy 1980; Edwards 1979; Cheshire 1982a). While these groups differ from each other in certain crucial ways, they have the following characteristics in common:

1. EITHER they live near each other in a recognised neighbourhood (such discrete homogeneous communities are sometimes called 'ghettoes');
   OR they have recognised meeting places (e.g. adolescents meet on waste ground, in adventure playgrounds, etc.).

2. They have a recognisable and distinctive sub-culture.

3. Members of the group acknowledge the existence of the group: belonging to the group is part of their identity.

Note that members of the majority group satisfy these conditions as well. Areas like Hampstead in London, or Clifton in Bristol for example, are sometimes called 'middle-class ghettoes', and it goes without saying that the majority group has a distinctive culture. Since this group is the dominant group, it is unmarked with respect to the other groups (in other words, perceived as normal or neutral, while other groups are 'marked' precisely because they differ from this norm). As a result, the majority culture is often considered to be *the* culture of society at large (just as Standard English is seen as *the* English language).

Women and men are peculiar as far as social groups go because in our society they tend to live in pairs consisting of one woman and one man: they certainly never live in separate areas as in (1.) above, except in special circumstances. 'Unlike many minority groups, women are not forced to live closely together in conditions conducive to the development of a collective group consciousness' (Williams & Giles 1978:436fn.). Moreover, where other groups define themselves in relation to out-groups and often come into conflict with these groups (e.g. West Indians in relation to the white community, adolescents in relation to adults), women and men tend to view each other favourably. Perhaps most importantly, it is not clear how far sex is salient as a category to women or men. In the opposition male-female, male is the unmarked term and for men, therefore, social class may be a more salient category than sex.

As far as women are concerned, their awareness of themselves as a group seems to be growing. According to social psychologists, people derive social identity from their membership of various social groups, but it has been pointed out that that these groups only have meaning when they are compared with other groups. Henri Tajfel, a social psychologist who developed a theory of inter-group relations and social change (see Tajfel 1974; 1978; 1981), was particularly interested in groups whose members had a poor self-image. This happens when a group has inferior social status and is seen in negative terms by comparison with other groups. Since it can plausibly be argued that women *do* belong to a social group of this kind (in our society they are considered – overtly or covertly – to be inferior to men and thus to have lower status), then it will be enlightening to see what Tajfel's theory predicts about social groups in this position, and what light it throws on women's position in society today, and on women's linguistic usage.[2]

Tajfel argues that members of an inferior social group (a minority group in the sense defined above) can either accept or reject their inferior position in society. If they accept it, they will try to achieve self-esteem and a positive self-image by operating as individuals, not as a group. There are two possible strategies for such people: firstly, they can measure themselves against members of their own group, not members of the superior group; secondly, they can try individually to join the superior group. If, on the other hand, they refuse to accept their inferior position in society as just, they will attempt as a group to change things. Tajfel outlines three ways they can do this (these strategies usually occur, historically, in the order given). Firstly, they will try to gain equality with and will adopt the values of the superior (majority) group; this strategy is called **assimilation**. Secondly, they will try to redefine characteristics which have previously been defined in negative terms by society; they will try to give these characteristics a positive value. Thirdly, they will try to create new dimensions for comparison with the superior group, so that they are defining for themselves what has positive value, and thereby creating a positive and distinct image for themselves. Figure 1.1 summarises this theory in diagrammatic form.

How far does the theory correspond to the reality of women's position in society today? In the past, women seemed to accept their inferior status; they allowed themselves to be defined by the

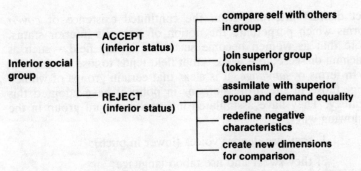

Figure 1.1: Tajfel's theory of inter-group relations and social change

superior group and they accepted this definition as just. This is still true of many women today. In order to achieve a positive self-image, such women compare themselves *with other women*. The relevant dimensions for comparison are things like cooking, sewing, child-care and personal appearance. The women's magazine industry is kept in business by this need for **intra-group** comparison (comparison with others in the same group). These women avoid comparing themselves with men. Occasionally, a woman who accepts inferior status for women as a group will attempt individually to leave the women's group and become accepted by men. (This strategy is clearly problematic for groups like women or blacks who are physically distinct from other groups; but for working-class groups, for example, it is a well-known strategy.) This occurs from time to time in business circles or in politics – a woman operates successfully in the men's world and becomes, to all intents and purposes, a man. However, this is a strategy which can achieve nothing for the group as a whole, but only for the individual. It can be called tokenism.

Nowadays women are more aware that they do not have equal status with men, and they are less prepared to accept this state of affairs. Do their attempts to change things fit Tajfel's theory? We will take the three predicted strategies in turn, and assess each one in relation to women's behaviour in general and their linguistic behaviour in particular.

Assimilation

This is clearly a strategy that is being pursued by women. There has been progress in terms of gaining equality in working conditions and in legal terms: the Equal Pay Act was passed in 1970 and the Sex Discrimination Act in 1975 – the Equal Opportunities Commission was set up to ensure the effective enforcement of these acts. Williams and Giles (1978) comment however that the effort involved in changing *overt* norms may in

WOMEN, MEN AND LANGUAGE

fact distract attention from the continued existence of *covert* norms which perpetuate the notion of women's inferior status. Note that as women become successful in any field – such as teaching or secretarial work – that field tends to lose status.

In terms of *language*, it is clear that certain groups of women (e.g. those in the professions or in politics) have adopted this strategy. They have assimilated into the dominant group in the following ways:

1. they use deeper voices (lower in pitch);
2. they swear and use taboo language;
3. they adopt a more assertive style in group interaction;
4. they adopt prosodic features more typical of men (e.g. falls rather than rising intonation patterns);
5. they address themselves in public to traditionally male topics: business, politics, economics;
6. they are beginning to exploit the use of non-standard accents (BBC employment patterns are a good guide in this area).

The problem with this strategy is that it means that women redefine themselves in terms of *male* values (the values of the dominant group). If women are searching for a satisfactory identity of their own, this is obviously a flawed strategy.

Redefinition of negative characteristics

This strategy is better known in relation to other minority groups, with the most telling example being the slogan *Black is Beautiful*. The positive valuation of what was previously labelled 'bad' also has clear linguistic correlates: note for example the upsurge in the use of West Indian based creoles among black adolescents in Britain, and the importance of the Welsh language to Welsh separatists.

Changing a negative image into a positive one is a very slow process. Some women are beginning to stress the *value* to society of stereotyped female qualities such as gentleness, caring for others, sensitivity. At the same time, they point out that stereotyped male qualities such as assertiveness, aggression, competitiveness, are not always socially useful. The concept of androgyny (an integration of male and female roles) has been advocated.[3] In linguistic terms, this strategy is still very new. Some women are challenging the use of *he* and *man*, arguing that such words exclude women. As far as language use is concerned, the most significant move seems to be a reappraisal by women of the relative merits of co-operative as opposed to competitive strategies in conversation. Research carried out in this field suggests that men typically adopt a competitive style in conversation, treating their turn as a chance to overturn earlier speakers' contributions and to make their own point as forcibly as possible. Women on the other hand, in conversation with other women, typically adopt a co-operative mode: they add to rather than demolish other speakers' contributions, they are supportive of others, they tend not to interrupt each other (this research will be discussed in 6.5 and 9.2). Articles discussing this difference comment that women are beginning to value their style and to resent being forced to adopt the male mode in mixed interaction. (In such articles, terms like *gossip* are being redefined positively.) It seems that women's less assertive, more co-operative style in group interaction is being revalued positively by women speakers, and conversely, men's style is being criticised.

Creation of new dimensions for comparison

Again very recently, women have initiated and made public new modes of social organisation. The crucial aspect of such organisation is that there is no named leader or organiser. When, for example, the police or the press ask for the leaders or spokespersons of the many women's Peace Camps in Britain, they are baffled at being told that there are none. Social organisation of this kind clearly stems from the co-operative mode valued by women and described in its linguistic manifestation above. When groups of women meet – as a committee or an organising body – it is beginning to be common either for there to be no chair or for the chair to rotate randomly from one session to another. (Note that the words *chairman* and *spokesman* are completely taboo.) In other words, women are developing new organisational modes. These clearly involve different linguistic strategies from those required by the traditional male style of committee meeting, with its clearly defined leader, its agenda and minutes, its meticulously worked out rules ('standing orders'). The new women's mode is more anarchic, more creative, more flexible – at all events, different.

As we can see from this brief appraisal of women as a group in the light of Tajfel's theory, women are still in the early stages of the process of change. Not all women feel that their inferior position in society is unjust. Those who *do* feel their subordinate position is unjust are mostly involved in assimilation strategies: that is, they are working to change the law and other social structures to give women equality. As we have already pointed out, while such moves are probably an essential prerequisite for social change, the strategy of assimilation is not in the long run healthy for a group in search of a positive social identity, since assimilation essentially means accepting the norms of the dominant group. By refusing to accept men's definitions, and by redefining female characteristics *positively*, some women are moving on to Tajfel's second and third strategies. But the creation of a new positive identity to replace the old subordinate one is an extremely slow process – especially as the dominant group does not accept change passively but will inevitably try by various means to preserve its superior position.

1.4   WOMEN, MEN AND LANGUAGE

We have looked at the nature of social groups, at the nature of subordinate (minority) groups in particular, and at the ways in which they seek to change their status. We have looked specifically at women as a social group, at their position in society, and at changes currently taking place in women's position. As we have said, these changes are only just beginning. The reason so much space has been devoted to this assessment of women's and men's relative position in society is that sociolinguistics aims not only to describe linguistic variation and the social context in which such variation occurs, but also to show how linguistic differentiation reflects social structure. Sociolinguistic studies reveal that linguistic variation is not random but structured: structured linguistic variation is a direct consequence of the structured social variation found in the speech community.

The structured social variation found in the speech community can be interpreted in more than one way. Women as a social group are clearly *different* from men. As a minority group they can also be seen as *oppressed* and *marginalised* (see Breakwell 1979). The two main approaches to sex differences in language reflect these two views of women's status as a group. The first – the **difference** approach – emphasises the idea that women and men belong to separate sub-cultures. The linguistic differences in women's and men's speech are interpreted as reflecting these different sub-cultures. (Linguists who adopt this approach often talk about 'women's language' and 'men's language'.) The second – the **dominance** approach – sees women as an oppressed group and interprets linguistic differences in women's and men's speech as a reflection of men's dominance and women's subordination. Both approaches seem to yield valuable insights into the nature of sex differences in language, and many sociolinguists have adopted a compromise position (this should become apparent in the discussion of sociolinguistic work in subsequent chapters). The value of these two different approaches will be reviewed in Chapter 9.

This book will restrict itself to linguistic variation related to the sex of the speaker. It will describe differences found in the speech of women and men, and it will relate these linguistic differences to the social roles assigned to women and men in our society. Chapter 2 will expose our society's preconceptions about sex differences in language, while Chapter 3 will assess the contribution of anthropology and dialectology to the study of sex differences. Having dealt with work carried out before the establishment of linguistics as a discipline, we shall move on to look in detail at sociolinguistic analyses of sex differences in language: Chapter 4 will focus on quantitative sociolinguistic studies, Chapter 5 on studies involving the concept of social network. In Chapter 6 we shall look at those studies which examine women's and men's linguistic behaviour in the wider sense of communicative competence: this will include studies on interruptions and silences in conversation, on swearing and on politeness, on different styles in group interaction, among other things. These three central chapters will also try to deal with socio-functional explanations, since the data presented inevitably lead to the question 'Why?' Many explanations for linguistic sex differentiation have been suggested and these will be reviewed and discussed. The final part, entitled 'Causes and Consequences', will examine three related areas in detail: children's acquisition of sex-differentiated language (Chapter 7), the nature of linguistic change and the role of sex differences in promoting change (Chapter 8), and finally the social consequences of sex differences in language, looking especially at miscommunication between adults and at the use of language in the school setting (Chapter 9).

1.5   WRITER'S CAVEAT

We have no choice about our sex: each one of us is either male or female. You, reading this book, will bring to your reading a set of intuitions about what it is like to be a female speaker or a male speaker today. You will also have been socialised into a set of preconceptions about the nature of women and men in general and about female and male speakers in particular. You should be alert to these preconceptions and to your own necessarily partial viewpoint when sifting the evidence presented in this book. Also remember that it is not only you, the reader, who have preconceptions and prejudices – I, the writer, have them too, and so have the various scholars whose work on language I shall be referring to. Obviously, the pursuit of any discipline involves an attempt by scholars to rise above their preconceptions and to assess the data objectively. However, it is surely not cynical to say that pure objectivity – especially in an area like language and sex which is so close to all of us – is probably a chimaera.

As a first step to coming to terms with our preconceptions, and in order to assess which linguistic sex differences are fiction and which fact, we will look at the cultural mythology associated with sex differences in language. The next chapter will address itself directly to this subject, and is accordingly called 'Folklinguistics'.

NOTES

1 The term *gender* will be used in certain fixed phrases such as *gender identity*, *gender role*, where there is no possibility of ambiguity, and where no alternative phrase exists.

2 For social psychological aspects of the following discussion I am indebted to Williams & Giles' article on 'The changing status of women in society', (1978).

3 On the concept of androgyny, see Bem 1974; and Bem 1975.

Chapter Two

The historical background (I) – Folklinguistics and the early grammarians

2.1 INTRODUCTION

Differences between women and men have always been a topic of interest to the human species and supposed linguistic differences are often enshrined in proverbs:

> A woman's tongue wags like a lamb's tail. (England)
> Foxes are all tail and women are all tongue. (England – Cheshire)
> Ou femme y a, silence n'y a. (France)
> The North Sea will sooner be found wanting in water than a woman at a loss for a word. (Jutland)[1]

The comments of contemporary observers, recorded in diaries, letters, poems, novels, etc., also provide us with evidence of folklinguistic beliefs about sex differences in language. Beside these more casual observations we can place the work of the early grammarians. It is not always easy to draw a line between the former and the latter, since much work entitled 'grammar' is no more scientific in its approach to linguistic sex differences than the observations of 'ordinary' people. In other words, academics and scholars are as much the product of the times they live in as are non-academics, and their work on language can be as subject to prejudice and preconception as are the comments of lay people.

As we shall see, scholarly comments on sex differences in language reflect the ideas of their time. In some cases this tendency has led to startling contradictions. Such contradictions can be accounted for by assuming a general rule, which I shall call **The Androcentric Rule**: 'Men will be seen to behave linguistically in a way that fits the writer's view of what is desirable or admirable; women on the other hand will be blamed for any linguistic state or development which is regarded by the writer as negative or reprehensible.'

15

2.2 FOLKLINGUISTICS

In this chapter I shall survey writings from the Middle Ages up to the beginning of this century (that is, work written before the discipline of linguistics was established). Rather than survey the entire field, I shall focus on the following areas of interest: vocabulary, swearing and taboo words, grammar, literacy, pronunciation, and verbosity.

2.2.1 Vocabulary

Interest in the lexical and grammatical structure of the language, that is, in its vocabulary and grammar, was stimulated by the rise of Standard English. Once one variety of a language is selected as the standard, then the process of codification inevitably follows. Codification involves the writing of both dictionaries (dealing with the lexical items of a language) and grammars (dealing with the grammatical structure of a language). In England, the eighteenth century saw the publication of numerous dictionaries and grammars, all written in an attempt to reduce the language to rule, and to legislate on 'correct' usage.

Commentary on sex differences in vocabulary is quite widespread in eighteenth-century writings, as the following extracts will demonstrate. The passage below, written by Richard Cambridge for *The World* of 12 December 1754, implies that the ephemeral nature of women's vocabulary is associated with the unimportance of what they say:

> I must beg leave . . . to doubt the propriety of joining to the fixed and permanent standard of language a vocabulary of words which perish and are forgot within the compass of a year. That we are obliged to the ladies for most of these ornaments to our language, I readily acknowledge.
>
> (Cambridge 1754, as quoted in Tucker 1961:93)

Here we see an eighteenth-century gentleman grappling with the problem of linguistic change. The ultimate aim of codification was to 'fix' the language once and for all. However, vocabulary was an area which appeared to elude control. On what grounds Richard Cambridge judged women to be responsible for ephemeral words, we are not told.

Turning to the early twentieth century, we find Otto Jespersen, a Danish professor of English language, writing on the question of changing vocabulary. He asserts that it is *men* rather than women who introduce 'new and fresh expressions' and thus men who are 'the chief renovators of language' (Jespersen 1922:247). This apparent inconsistency can be accounted for by the Androcentric Rule (see 2.1). As the rule would predict, in an age which

16

deplored lexical change, women were held to be the culprits for introducing ephemeral words. On the other hand, Jespersen in 1922 accepted that change was inevitable and saw innovation as creative: he therefore credited men with introducing new words to the lexicon.

An anonymous contributor to *The World* (6 May 1756) complains of women's excessive use of certain adverbial forms:

> Such is the pomp of utterance of our present women of fashion; which, though it may tend to spoil many a pretty mouth, can never recommend an indifferent one. And hence it is that there is so great a scarcity of originals, and that the ear is such a daily sufferer from an identity of phrase, whether it be *vastly, horridly, abominably, immensely*, or *excessively*, which, with three or four more calculated for the same swiss-like service, make up the whole scale or gamut of modern female conversation.
> (as quoted in Tucker 1961:96)

This characteristic women's language is gently mocked by Jane Austen in *Northanger Abbey* (1813), in the speech of Isabella Thorpe:

> 'My attachments are always *excessively* strong.'
> 'I must confess there is something *amazingly* insipid about her'
> 'I am so vexed with all the men for not admiring her! – I scold them all *amazingly* about it'.
> (*Northanger Abbey*, Ch. 6, my italics)

It is clearly significant that it is Isabella, who is flirtatious, selfish and shallow, who uses these adverbials, and not Catherine, the heroine (who is altogether less sophisticated).

The use of adverbial forms of this kind was a fashion at this time, and was evidently associated in the public mind with women's speech. Lord Chesterfield, writing in *The World* of 5 December 1754, makes very similar observations to those of the anonymous contributor quoted above:

> Not content with enriching our language with words absolutely new [*again the accusation that women destabilise the lexicon*] my fair countrywomen have gone still farther, and improved it by the application and extension of old ones to various and very different significations. They take a word and change it, like a guinea, into shillings for pocket money, to be employed in the several occasional purposes of the day. For instance, the adjective *vast* and it's (*sic*) adverb *vastly*, mean anything and are the fashionable words of the most fashionable people. A fine woman ... is *vastly* obliged, or *vastly* offended, *vastly* glad or *vastly* sorry. Large objects are *vastly* great, small ones are *vastly* little; and I had lately the pleasure to hear a fine woman

pronounce, by a happy metonymy, a very small gold snuff-box that was produced in company to be *vastly* pretty, because it was *vastly* little.
(as quoted in Tucker 1961:92)

Lord Chesterfield concludes with a mock-serious appeal to one of the great legislators of the time, Dr Johnson, whose *Dictionary* (1755) was a landmark in the codification process. 'Mr. Johnson', Lord Chesterfield says, 'will do well to consider seriously to what degree he will restrain the various and extensive significants of this great word' [i.e. *vast*].

Johnson's *Dictionary* is well known for its individualistic and biased definitions (*Patron* is defined as 'Commonly a wretch who supports with insolence, and is paid with flattery'). Johnson stigmatises the words *flirtation* and *frightful* as 'female cant'. Such a comment is value-laden. It seems clear that the anonymous contributor to *The World* quoted above is a man: all these passages reveal that their (male) authors believe women to have restricted and vacuous vocabulary, and to exert a malign influence on the language. Note that 'language' is defined by these eighteenth-century writers in terms of male language; the way men talk is seen as the norm, while women's language is deviant.

The androcentric bias is still present in twentieth-century observations on English vocabulary. Jespersen included a chapter entitled 'The Woman' in his book *Language: Its Nature, Development and Origin* (1922). This chapter has the merit of summarising extant research on women's language in many different parts of the world. It has been justifiably criticised, however, for its uncritical acceptance of sexist assumptions about male/female differences in language. Jespersen includes a section on vocabulary in this chapter. He generalises that 'the vocabulary of a woman as a rule is much less extensive than that of a man'. He supports this claim with data from an experiment by an American, Jastrow, in which male college students used a greater variety of words than female college students when asked to write down one hundred (separate) words. This is the only evidence given.

In his section on adverbs, Jespersen says that woman differ from men in their extensive use of certain adjectives, such as *pretty* and *nice*. It should be noted that the American linguist, Robin Lakoff, in *Language and Woman's Place*, the work that for many people marks the beginning of twentieth-century linguistic interest in sex differences, specifically singles out '"empty" adjectives like *divine, charming, cute . . .*' as typical of what she calls 'women's language' (Lakoff 1975:53).

Women differ from men, according to Jespersen, even more in their use of adverbs. Quoting Lord Chesterfield's remarks on the adverb *vastly* (see above), Jespersen argues that this is 'a distinctive trait: the fondness of women for hyperbole will very often lead the fashion with regard to adverbs of intensity, and these are very often used with disregard of their proper meaning' (Jespersen 1922:250). (This of course begs the question of 'proper' meaning.) He quotes examples from all the major European languages. This proves that adverbs are widely used in these speech communities, but we are given no evidence to show that it is only, or preponderantly, women who use them.

So is also claimed as having 'something of the eternally feminine about it'. Jespersen quotes *Punch* of 4 January 1896: 'This little adverb is a great favourite with ladies, in conjunction with an adjective'. The extract gives as examples of 'ladies usage': 'It is *so* lovely!'; 'he is *so* charming!'; 'Thank you *so* much!'; 'I'm *so* glad you've come!' Jespersen's 'explanation' for this sex-preferential usage is that 'women much more often than men break off without finishing their sentences, because they start talking without having thought out what they are going to say . . . ' (Jespersen 1922:250).

Lakoff also has a section on the intensifier *so*. She asserts that '*so* is more frequent in women's than men's language, though certainly men can use it' (Lakoff 1975:54). As we shall see in subsequent sections, there are many parallels between Lakoff's and Jespersen's work, which is surprising in view of the fact that feminists welcomed Lakoff's book, but have been very critical of Jespersen's.

2.2.2 Swearing and taboo language

'A whistling sailor, a crowing hen and a swearing woman ought all three to go to hell together'.
(American proverb)

In this section I shall be considering oaths, exclamations, taboo words: anything which could come under the general heading 'vulgar language'. The belief that women's language is more polite, more refined – in a word, more ladylike – is very widespread and has been current for many centuries.

Vulgarity is a cultural construct, and the evidence suggests that it was the new courtly tradition of the Middle Ages which, by creating gentility, also created vulgarity. The issue of vulgar language forms an important theme of French *fabliaux*, comic tales of the Middle Ages, which seem in part to have been written in direct response to the new vogue for 'clean' language. One – *La Dame qui se venja du Chevalier* (Montaiglon et Raynaud, 1872–90: vol VI) – explicitly supports the courtly taboo stigmatising a man's use of obscene language in front of a woman. The man and woman are in bed together when the man commits his faux pas: 'the knight, who was on top, looked right at her face and saw her swooning with pleasure. Whereupon he couldn't suppress his foolishness but said something very vulgar. Right then he asked her "My lady, would you crack some nuts?"' (as translated in Muscatine 1981:11). *Croistre noiz* (crack nuts) is a synonym for *foutre* (fuck). The woman is extremely offended and proceeds to take her revenge.

In contrast to this, there is a group of three *fabliaux* (the two versions of *La damoisele qui ne pooit oïr parler de foutre* and *la pucele qui abevra le polain*) which can be read as an attack on linguistic prudery in women, and which defend the use of vernacular ('vulgar') terms. In all three versions of the story, the heroine is a stuck-up (*dédaigneuse*) young woman who can't bear to hear any words to do with sex – they make her feel ill. The father can't keep male servants as they don't speak language suitable for his daughter's ears. The hero is a clever young man who arrives on the pretext of looking for work and feigns disgust at hearing obscene language, thus gaining the confidence of the father and daughter. The girl is so convinced of his purity that she invites him to sleep in her bed. A mutual seduction takes place, with the lovers using elaborate metaphors of ponies, meadows, fountains, etc. to avoid the use of taboo expressions. The writer comments in one version: 'I want to show by this example that women should not be too proud to say *foutre* (fuck) out loud when all the same they're doing it' (as translated in Muscatine 1981:14). The humour in these tales arises from the ludicrous contrast between the woman's dislike of the *words* and her pleasure in the *act*. A famous passage in the *Roman de la Rose* (c. 1277) attacks the use of euphemisms and circumlocutions, and calls for plain language. The writer comments: 'If women don't name them (i.e. *coilles*, bollocks) in France, it's nothing but getting out of the habit' (as quoted in Muscatine 1981:17). Presumably there have always been taboos on language, but it looks as if the courtly tradition of the Middle Ages, which put women on a pedestal, strengthened linguistic taboos in general, and also condemned the use of vulgar language by women, and its use by men in front of women.

The strength of the folklinguistic belief in male/female differences in swearing is reflected in Elyot's strictures on the upbringing of noblemen's children in *The Governour* (1531). Elyot advises that the child of a Gentleman should be brought up by women who will not permit 'any wanton or unclene worde to be spoken' in the child's presence. To avoid the child's hearing such words, he urges that no men should be allowed into the nursery.

Shakespeare on the other hand makes fun of this cultural stereotype. In *I Henry IV*, Hotspur mocks his wife for her genteel use of oaths:

Hotspur: Come, Kate, I'll have your song too.
Lady Percy: Not mine, in good sooth.
Hotspur: Not yours, 'in good sooth'! Heart! you swear like a
comfit-maker's wife! Not yours, 'in good sooth'; and 'as true as I
live'; and 'as God shall mend me'; and 'as sure as day';
And givst such sarcenet surety for thy oaths,
As if thou never walk'dst further than Finsbury.
Swear me, Kate, like a lady as thou art,
A good mouth-filling oath; and leave 'in sooth'
And such protest of pepper-gingerbread
To velvet-guards and Sunday citizens.
(*I Henry IV*, III. i. 248ff.)

Shakespeare here reveals an awareness that swearing is related not
only to sex but also to social class. Hotspur urges Kate to swear *not*
like a comfit-maker's wife and other 'Sunday citizens' (the
bourgeoisie), but like 'a lady', that is, a female member of the
aristocracy.

As the previous section has shown, eighteenth-century
gentlemen were having to come to terms with the fact of linguistic
change. Arthur Murphy, in a witty article in *Gray's Inn Journal* of
29 June 1754, suggests that there should be a Register of Births
and Deaths for words. He elaborates on this idea with the
following conceit:

A Distinction might be made between a kind of Sex in Words,
according as they are appropriated to Men or Women; as for
Instance, *D--n my Blood* is of Male extraction, and *Pshaw,
Fiddlestick* I take to be female . . .
(as quoted in Tucker 1961:86)

The idea of distinct male and female swear words is still widely
held. Lakoff, two-hundred years later, makes exactly the same
observation as Murphy; she says:

'Consider (a) "Oh dear, you've put the peanut butter in the
               refrigerator again."
         (b) "Shit, you've put the peanut butter in the
               refrigerator again."
It is safe to predict that people would classify the first sentence
as part of "women's language", the second as "men's
language".'
(Lakoff 1975:10)

Lakoff summarises her position later by saying 'women don't use
off-color or indelicate expressions; women are the experts at
euphemism' (op. cit:55).
While noting that she is talking about 'general tendencies'

21

rather than 'hundred-percent correlations', Lakoff seems happy to present such folklinguistic material without the support of any research findings to confirm or refute her statements. It is less surprising that Jespersen, in 1922, held such views:

> There can be no doubt that women exercise a great and universal influence on linguistic development through their instinctive shrinking from coarse and gross expressions and their preference for refined and (in certain spheres) veiled and indirect expressions.

He goes on to the particular case of swearing:

> Among the things women object to in language must be specially mentioned anything that smacks of swearing.

In a footnote to this, he adds:

> There are great differences with regard to swearing between different nations; but I think that in those countries and in those circles in which swearing is common it is found much more extensively among men than among women: this at any rate is true of Denmark.
>
> (Jespersen 1922:246)

These writers claim to describe women's more polite use of language, but we should ask whether what they are actually doing is attempting to prescribe how women *ought to* talk. Avoidance of swearing and of 'coarse' words is held up to female speakers as the ideal to be aimed at (as is silence, as we shall see in the section on Verbosity). It is clear that people have thought for a long time that women and men differ in relation to the use of swear words and other taboo expressions. As Chapter 6 (6.2.2) will show, there is still very little evidence to confirm or refute this belief.

2.2.3 Grammar

The rise of Standard English stimulated an awareness of variation in language and with it the growth of the notion of correctness. Once a standard was accepted and codified, then forms which deviated from this standard were frowned on as 'incorrect'. Eighteenth-century notions of grammar were less sophisticated than today's: grammars were prescriptive rather than descriptive, laying down rules of correct usage. They often included sections on spelling and punctuation, which demonstrates how early grammarians took the *written* language as the basis for their work.

The earliest writers on grammar and rhetoric were concerned about the 'correct' ordering of elements in phrases such as *men and women*:

22

> Some will set the Carte before the horse, as thus, My mother and my father are both at home, even as thoughe the good man of the house ware no breaches, or that the graye Mare were the better Horse. And what thoughe it often so happeneth (God wotte the more pitte) yet in speaking at the least, let us kepe a natural order, and set the man before the woman for maners Sake.
>
> (Wilson 1560:189)

This idea of 'a natural order' and of the superiority of the male is unabashedly prescribed for linguistic usage: 'The Masculine gender is more worthy than the Feminine' (Poole 1646:21). This idea seems to have been a necessary precursor of the sex-indefinite *he* rule, which proscribes the use of *they* or *he or she* where the sex of the antecedent is unknown. Compare the following three sentences:

1. Someone knocked at the door but they had gone when I got downstairs.

2. Someone knocked at the door but he or she had gone when I got downstairs.

3. Someone knocked at the door but he had gone when I got downstairs.

According to prescriptive grammarians, only the last of these three utterances is 'correct' (the first is 'incorrect' and the second 'clumsy'). John Kirkby's statement, from his *New English Grammar* of 1746, is the one most frequently quoted:

> The Masculine Person answers to the general Name, which comprehends both Male and Female; as *Any Person, who knows what he says.*
>
> (Kirkby 1746:117)

This is not the place for a full discussion of the rival merits of generic *he* and singular *they* in contexts requiring a sex-indefinite pronoun (for a detailed account, see Bodine 1975b). The important point is that the androcentric (male-as-norm) attitudes so conspicuous in early pronouncements on language were actually used as the basis for some prescriptive rules of grammar. Many people will see feminist opposition to the use of sex-indefinite *he* as misguided and doomed to failure ('I feel . . . that an attempt to change pronominal usage will be futile'; Lakoff 1975:45). What these people are unaware of is the fact that the present rule was itself imposed on language users by male grammarians of the eighteenth century and after. It is naïve to assume that codification was carried out in a disinterested fashion: those who laid down the rules inevitably defined as 'correct' that usage which they preferred, for whatever reason.

Observations on language by men of letters reveal an assumption that women are frequently guilty of incorrect usage, as far as grammar is concerned. The following passage is typical of its time:

> I came yesterday into the Parlour, where I found Mrs. Cornelia, my lady's third Daughter, all alone, reading a Paper, which, as I afterwards found, contained a Copy of Verses, upon Love and Friendship . . . . By the Hand [i.e. *handwriting*], at first sight, I could not guess whether they came from a Lady, but having put on my spectacles, and perused them carefully, I found by some peculiar Modes in Spelling, and a certain Negligence in Grammar, that it was a Female Sonnet.

(Richard Steele 1713; as quoted in Tucker 1961:69)

Lord Chesterfield (1741) remarks: 'most women and all the ordinary people in general speak in open defiance of all grammar'. Henry Tilney tells Catherine Morland that: 'the usual style of letter writing among women is faultless, except in three particulars' which are 'a general deficiency of subject, a total inattention to stops, and a very frequent ignorance of grammar' (*Northanger Abbey* 1813). Although he is teasing, we can assume that these were the kind of taunts about grammatical incorrectness which were commonly made at women's expense at the time.

Jespersen inevitably has much to say on the subject of grammar and male/female differences. As we have seen (in relation to *so*, 2.2.1), he believed that women often produce half-finished sentences (as a result of not thinking before speaking!). He claims that this happens particularly with exclamatory sentences, and he illustrates his claim with the following examples (both taken from literature):

> "Mrs. Eversleigh: I must say!" (but words fail her).
> (Hankin, quoted in Jespersen 1922:251)
> "The trouble you must have taken," Hilda exclaimed.
> (Compton-MacKenzie, quoted in Jespersen 1922:251)

These utterances are precisely the kind of thing that real people, of both sexes, do say. The concept of the half-finished sentence results from treating written language as primary. The sentence is the main unit of written language, but analysis of spoken discourse (a relatively new pursuit) suggests that the sentence may not be a relevant category for speech. However, since in the past men received far more education than women, it is likely that their speech was more affected by written norms; in other words, male/female differences may have reflected relative exposure to written language. But we have no quantitative evidence to support this hypothesis.

Jespersen's second claim revolves around the concepts of **parataxis** and **hypotaxis**. Clauses can be joined together in a variety of ways. **Parataxis** is the term used to describe a sequence of clauses where there are no links at all (the clauses are simply juxtaposed): CLAUSE, CLAUSE (e.g. *I got up*, *I went to work*). Similar to this, but not always included in the term 'parataxis', is **co-ordination**, where the clauses are linked by **co-ordinating** conjunctions (*and*, *but*, etc.): CLAUSE and CLAUSE (e.g. *I got up* and *I went to work*). **Hypotaxis** is the term used to describe a sequence of clauses where the links are **subordinating** conjunctions (*after*, *when*, *because*, etc): after CLAUSE, CLAUSE/ CLAUSE after CLAUSE (e.g. After *I got up*, *I went to work*/ *I went to work* after *I got up*).

The crucial difference between these two modes is that parataxis involves a series of main clauses, each clause being of equal value, while hypotaxis consists of a main clause with one or more subordinate clauses dependent on it. The logical connections between the clauses are made *explicit* in a hypotactic style, but left *implicit* in a paratactic style.

There is a long tradition in our culture of scorning parataxis and praising hypotaxis. Paratactic constructions tend to be called 'primitive', presumably because of their surface-structure lack of logical connectives. Hypotactic constructions, on the other hand, are universally admired, especially from the Renaissance onwards. It should be remembered that the classic Latin sentence involves complex subordination, and classical models were revered.

Jespersen's analysis of male/female differences in syntax makes use of this distinction:

> If we compare long periods [= *sentences*] as constructed by men and by women, we shall in the former find many more instances of intricate or involute structures with clause within clause, a relative clause in the middle of a conditional clause or vice versa, with subordination and sub-subordination, while the typical form of long feminine periods is that of co-ordination, one sentence or clause being added to another on the same plane and the gradation between the respective ideas being marked not grammatically, but emotionally, by stress and intonation, and in writing by underlining. In learned terminology we may say that men are fond of hypotaxis and women of parataxis.
> (Jespersen 1922:251)

The distinction between *grammatically* and *emotionally* is obscure, but *emotionally* is presumably pejorative, and suggests that Jespersen finds the hypotactic style superior. He continues with two famous similes:

'a male period is often like a set of Chinese boxes, one within another, while a feminine period is like a set of pearls joined together on a string of *ands* and similar words.'
(op. cit.:252)

At his most sexist, Jespersen is still a gentleman!

More recently, the paratactic/hypotactic distinction has been used to distinguish between Bernstein's restricted and elaborated codes.[2] Without using these terms, Bernstein appeals to our culturally conditioned notion that hypotaxis is a superior mode of construction: he claims that subordination is typical of elaborated code, while restricted code makes use of 'simple' co-ordinated clauses. Linguists agree that there is nothing intrinsically superior about a construction involving subordinate clauses, but note that hypotactic constructions are typical of written language, while paratactic constructions are typical of speech. We can draw up a simple table (Table 2.1) to show the correspondences.

Table 2.1: The linguistic domains (real and hypothesised) of parataxis and hypotaxis

	Parataxis	Hypotaxis
Typically found in:	Anglo-Saxon prose	Renaissance and post-Renaissance prose
	Speech	Writing
Supposed to be typical of:	Restricted code	Elaborated code
	Women's language	Men's language

As has been said earlier, there has been a tendency for scholars to measure everything against the benchmark of formal written prose. Both Jespersen's claims about women's syntax seem to relate to differences between the spoken and written language. Written language (in particular, printed material) was produced mostly by men (see 2.2.4); this means that Jespersen could judge men on their written syntax but he was more likely to have judged women's syntax on the basis of their spoken language.

2.2.4 Literacy

This section is closely linked to the preceding one. There is no doubt that until the coming of state education for all in this century, women had less access to literacy than men. Before the nineteenth century, only women of the middle class and above were likely to be literate, and even then, when we say literate, we mean literate in the vernacular. The brothers and husbands of these same women were literate in the classical languages as well.

Classical Latin and Greek were no longer spoken as mother-tongues by anyone: they survived as languages only in the male world of the school, the university and the church. When Milton was asked whether he would teach his daughters other languages, he is alleged to have replied: 'One tongue is sufficient for a woman'.

The following extract shows that, while seventeenth- and eighteenth-century gentlemen agreed that women's language had its defects, especially their written language, they were not all opposed to the idea of changing this state of affairs through education. The extract is taken from the introduction to a work entitled *The Many Advantages of a Good Language to any Nation: with an Examination of the Present State of our own: As also, An Essay towards correcting some Things that are wrong in it.* This work has been ascribed to Thomas Wilson (1663–1755), Bishop of Sodor and Man. After emphasising the Power of Words, the writer warns that an improper use of words reflects badly on the user.

> We could heartily wish that the fair sex would take notice of this last Reason; for many a pretty Lady by the Silliness of her Words, hath lost the Admiration which her Face had gained. And as the Mind hath more lovely and more lasting Charms than the Body, if they would captivate Men of Sense, they must not neglect those best kind of Beauties. As these Perfections do not depend upon the Strength of the Hand, but the Quickness of the Wit, and Niceness of the Eye and Ear; and as in these Talents Nature hath doubtless been as bountiful to that Sex as to our own, those improprieties in Words, Spelling and Writing, for which they are usually laughed at, are not owing to any Defect in their Minds, but the Carelessness, if not Injustice to them in their Education. These following Essays are intended for a Help to them as well as others.
> (Wilson? 1724:37)

He goes on to point out the importance of educating the mothers of the nation's children. We can all admire the liberality of his sentiments, while noting that he addresses his remarks exclusively to men ('. . . Nature has doubtless been as bountiful to that Sex as to our own. . . .'). At the time this was written (1724), women's writing was clearly the subject of mockery; moreover, women obviously received very little and very poor education. Swift makes the same point, with typical exaggeration, in his *A Letter to a Young Lady on her Marriage* (1727):

> It is a little hard that not one Gentleman's daughter in a thousand should be brought to read or understand her own natural tongue, or be judge of the easiest Books that are written in it.

Henry Tilney's teasing of Catherine about women's letter writing, quoted in the previous section, shows that little had changed nearly a century later.

Rousseau (1712–78) condemns women's writing, but on different grounds from those we have heard so far. He says:

> . . . that burning eloquence, those sublime raptures which transmit delight to the very foundation of the soul will always be lacking from women's writings. They are all cold and pretty like their authors. They may show great wit but never any soul.
> (Rousseau, *La Lettre d'Alembert sur les Spectacles*, as translated by Peggy Kamuf 1980:290)

In the Romantic Age, then, women are seen as inferior because their writings lack passion. We can contrast this with Jespersen's claim that women prefer paratactic modes of expression (see 2.2.3), a claim which rests on the assertion that they are 'emotional' where men are 'grammatical'. This contradiction is more easily understood if we take the view that each era redefines what is admirable in language and what is to be avoided (**The Androcentric Rule**). There is consistency in Rousseau's and Jespersen's finding that women are performing less admirably than men.

It is not until this century that we can take it for granted that women are literate, that women have equal access to education, and that women's voices are heard equally with men's (at least in theory). Women's comments on writing give us an insight into the problems of using a medium which has over the centuries been in the hands of men. Virginia Woolf is particularly concerned with the form of the written sentence:

> But it is still true that before a woman can write exactly as she wishes to write, she has many difficulties to face. To begin with, there is the technical difficulty – so simple, apparently; in reality, so baffling – that the very form of the sentence does not fit her. It is a sentence made by men; it is too loose, too heavy, too pompous for a woman's use. Yet in a novel, which covers so wide a stretch of ground, an ordinary and usual type of sentence has to be found to carry the reader on easily and naturally from one end of the book to the other. And this a woman must make for herself, altering and adapting the current sentence until she writes one that takes the natural shape of her thought without crushing or distorting it.
> (Woolf 1929, as published in Woolf 1979:48)

While some will dispute the sexist idea that a woman's thoughts are a different shape from a man's and therefore need a different form of expression, no one will deny that written language, before the development of the novel, had been a male preserve. Men who

28

wrote had been trained in Rhetoric and exposed to traditional patterns of thinking and expression. Whether this entailed any particular type of sentence – loose, heavy, pompous, presumably influenced by classical models – is a matter which requires detailed examination. However, the growing literacy of women has clearly not been unproblematic. Women's difficulties with the written language seem more often to have been the butt of male wit, rather than the subject of sympathetic understanding.

2.2.5 Pronunciation

The rise of a standard variety of written English was followed by the rise of a standard variety of *spoken* English. After the development of a standard grammar and lexicon, the need was felt for a standard in pronunciation. The accent normally associated with standard English is R.P. (Received Pronunciation), an accent which differs from all other English accents in that it is no longer associated with any particular geographical region. The growth of a spoken standard is accompanied by the growth of ideas about what constitutes 'good' speech. As the educated speech of the Court in London became prestigious, so other accents began to be stigmatised. Comments by contemporary writers reveal again an androcentric view of linguistic usage with women's speech singled out as deviating from the (male) norms.

Elyot, in *The Governour* (1531), gives the following advice on the subject of nurses and other women who look after noblemen's children when they are infants:

> [they shall] at the lest way ... speke none English but that which is cleane, polite, perfectly and articulately pronounced, omittinge no lettre or sillable, as folisshe women oftentimes do of a wantonnesse, whereby divers noblemen and gentilmennes chyldren (as I do at this daye knowe) have attained corrupte and foul pronuntiation.
> (Elyot 1531)

Note that the appeal to the idea that no letters or syllables should be omitted is an appeal to the notion of written language as norm. As we have seen, in the section on grammar, spoken English has been compared with written ever since the growth of a written standard. Where writing and speech differ (and we are only now beginning to understand how great these differences are), there has been a tendency to see the spoken form as incorrect, or as deviating from the ideal. The above passage reminds us again that gentlemen, as the educated literate group in society, had a different view of language from women.

The following extract (taken from Gill's *Logonomia Anglica* 1619–21) links the speech of women with that of low-status men:

29

in speech the custom of the learned is the first law. Writing therefore is to be adjusted, not to that sound which herds-men, girls [*mulierculae*] and porters use; but to that which the learned or cultivated scholars [*docti aut culte eruditi viri*] use in speaking and recitation.
(as translated in Dobson 1969:435, fn4)

The pronunciation of female speakers (*mulierculae*) is explicitly compared with that of male speakers (*viri*), and readers are urged to imitate educated *men*. The grouping of herdsmen, porters and girls together shows us that prestigious speech was clearly associated with education. It is not clear, however, whether women and men of the same social class in the seventeenth century *did* talk differently – it is only this century that quantitative sociolinguistic analysis has been applied to speech.

Jespersen includes an excellent survey of male/female differences in pronunciation in his chapter on 'The Woman', in a section oddly entitled 'Phonetics and Grammar' (where is the grammar?). He interprets the comments of early grammarians as showing that women had a more advanced pronunciation than men. For example, he quotes Mulcaster (1582): '*Ai* is the man's diphthong, and soundeth full: *ei*, the woman's, and soundeth finish (i.e. fineish) in the same both sense, and use, *a woman is deintie, and feinteth soon, the man fainteth not bycause he is nothing daintie*'. Jespersen comments: 'Thus what is now distinctive of refined as opposed to vulgar pronunciation was then characteristic of the fair sex' (Jespersen 1922:243). He demonstrates that this tendency to innovate was not confined to English women, giving examples from France, Denmark and even Siberia. He devotes a paragraph to 'the weakening of the old fully trilled tongue-point r' (op. cit.:244). He argues that this change, which has occurred in many languages, has been brought about to a large extent by women. His evidence is slight, and his explanation bizarre: 'The old trilled point sound is natural and justified when life is chiefly carried on out-of-doors, but indoor life prefers, on the whole, less noisy speech habits' (op. cit.:244). He argues, in effect, that sounds which are appropriate in a rural setting are inappropriate in an urban one. His observation of differences between the speech of 'the great cities' and 'the rustic population' seems plausible, but his correlation of city life with 'refined domestic life' (and therefore under women's influence) seems naïve.

Writing in 1922, Jespersen concludes with the statement: 'In present-day English there are said to be a few differences in pro-nunciation between the two sexes.' They are listed in Table 2.2 as he gives them (the first two are attributed to Daniel Jones, who was Professor of Phonetics at London University). It is

Table 2.2: Sex differences in pronunciation in England, 1922 (based on Jespersen 1922:245)

Men	Women	
[sɔ:ft]	[sɔft]	*soft*
[gə:l]	[gɛəl]	*girl*
[waɪt]	[hwaɪt]	*white*
[tʃɪldrən]	[tʃʊldrən]	*children*
['weskət]	['weɪs'koʊt]	*waistcoat*

interesting to note that, while Jespersen here demonstrates differences in women's and men's pronunciation, his examples, if accurate, do not reveal a consistent pattern: the more 'advanced' forms – [sɔft], [gə:l], [waɪt], [tʃɪldrən] and [weɪskoʊt] – are not correlated with sex.

Jespersen concludes that these are isolated instances – 'on the whole we must say that from a phonetic point of view there is scarcely any difference between the speech of men and that of women: the two sexes speak for all intents and purposes the same language' (Jespersen 1922:245). However, his earlier observations on women's more advanced pronunciation have been borne out by much twentieth-century work in sociolinguistics. The relationship between women's speech and linguistic change will be pursued in Chapter 8.

2.2.6 Verbosity

> Many women, many words; many geese, many turds
> (English proverb)

There is an age-old belief that women talk too much. The cultural myth of women's verbosity is nicely caught in this fifteenth-century carol which describes the many virtues of women, but undermines the message with a refrain telling us that the opposite is true:

> Of all creatures women be best
> Cuius contrarium verum est. [*of which the opposite is true*]
> (Davies 1963:222)

Women are described as 'not liberal in language but ever in secree'. The reader is encouraged to confide in women:

> For tell a woman all your counsaile
> And she can kepe it wonderly well.

The writer, tongue in cheek, defends women against the charge of being chatterboxes:

> Trow ye that women list to smater [*chatter*]
> Or against their husbondes for to clater?

Nay! they had lever fast, bred and water,
Then for to dele in suche a matter.

The humour of this poem derives from the reader knowing that the writer intends the opposite meaning throughout. Since the key to understanding this joke is the Latin phrase in the refrain, the joke is clearly a male one, since Latin and Greek were taught only to boys (see the section on Literacy, 2.2.4).

English literature is filled with characters who substantiate the stereotype of the talkative woman. Rosalind, in *As You Like It* (III.2.264) says: 'Do you not know I am a woman? When I think, I must speak'. Dion, in Beaumont and Fletcher's *Philaster* (II.4.1–3) advises:

Come, ladies, shall we talk a round? As men
Do walk a mile, women should talk an hour
After supper; 'tis their exercise.

While Aurora Leigh, the eponymous heroine of Elizabeth Barrett Browning's poem of 1856, says: 'A woman's function plainly is – to talk.'

In a section on 'the volubility of women', Jespersen quotes examples from literature such as those above to prove his point, and refers to research done on reading speed which found that women tended to read a given passage faster than men and to remember more about the passage after reading it. In the face of this evidence, Jespersen asserts: 'But it was found that this rapidity was no proof of intellectual power, and some of the slowest readers were highly distinguished men'! (Jespersen 1922:252). To support his prejudice, Jespersen refers to Havelock Ellis's work *Man and Woman* (1894), which 'explains' that 'with the quick reader it is as though every statement were admitted immediately and without inspection to fill the vacant chambers of the mind' (op. cit.:252), and to Swift's assertion that:

the common fluency of speech in many men, and most women, is owing to the scarcity of matter, and scarcity of words; for whoever is a master of language, and hath a mind full of ideas, will be apt in speaking to hesitate upon the choice of both: whereas common speakers have only one set of ideas, and one set of words to clothe them in; and these are always ready at the mouth.
(Swift, op.cit.:252)

It must be obvious to any reader today that none of this represents a valid argument. Jespersen obviously accepts the cultural stereotype of the voluble chattering woman; he presents us with some tangential data on reading speed; he then argues that women's facility with words does not correspond to any intellectual power (but rather the contrary), and quotes the dogmatic statements of two famous men, as if this constituted supporting evidence. Since he provides no data on the speed and quantity of women's speech, the passage tells us nothing except that scholars of language in the early part of this century were subject to the prejudices of their times.

The other side of the coin to women's verbosity is the image of the silent woman which is often held up as an ideal – 'Silence is the best ornament of a woman' (English proverb). This ideal is found very early in literary texts, for example, in the Arthurian romances, in stories such as Erec and Enyd. This exists in versions by Chrétien de Troyes (c. 1170), in *The Mabinogion* (c. 1300), and in Tennyson's *Idylls of the King* (1859). The crucial episode involves Erec (Geraint in *The Mabinogion*/Tennyson) and Enyd riding alone on a journey during which Erec tests his wife's loyalty to him. Erec says:

> and this
> I charge thee, on thy duty as a wife,
> Whatever happens, not to speak to me,
> No, not a word!
> (Tennyson, *Geraint and Enid*)

Silence is made synonymous with obedience.

The tale of Patient Griselda also appears in many different forms, for example, as 'The Clerk's Tale' in Chaucer's *Canterbury Tales*. Again, a wife's loyalty and obedience are tested – this time her children are forcibly taken from her. Even though Griselda believes they may be killed, she does not protest: 'Ne in this tyme word ne spak she noon' ('The Clerk's Tale', l. 900). Silence is again portrayed as intrinsic to obedience. (It should be noted that Griselda passes the test of obedience with flying colours, and is thus a character twentieth-century readers have difficulties with; Enyd on the other hand breaks her husband's command in order to warn him of danger – she saves his life by refusing to remain silent.)

During the Renaissance, eloquence was highly acclaimed, but Tasso, in his *Discorso della virtu feminile e donnesca* (1582), makes it clear that while eloquence is a virtue in a man, *silence* is the corresponding virtue in a woman. As one scholar comments: 'The implication is that it is inappropriate for a woman to be eloquent or liberal, or for a man to be economical and silent' (MacLean 1980:62).

The model of the silent woman is still presented to girls in the second half of the twentieth century: research in English schools suggests that quiet behaviour is very much encouraged by teachers, particularly in girls. This will be discussed at greater length in section 9.3.

Dale Spender comments on the issue of women and silence:

> The talkativeness of women has been gauged in comparison
> not with men but with *silence* . . . When silence is the desired
> state for women . . . then any talk in which a woman engages
> can be too much.
> (Spender 1980a:42)

Many linguists have dismissed Spender's views as extremist.
However, in relation to the specific topic of women's supposed
verbosity, this section has demonstrated that pre-Chomskyan
linguistic enquiry provides us with no *evidence* that women talked
more than men, yet there is no doubt that Western European
culture is imbued with the belief that women *do* talk a lot,[3] and
there is evidence that silence is an ideal that has been held up to
women for many centuries.

2.3 CONCLUSION

In this chapter we have looked at folklinguistic views of
male/female differences in language and those of the early
grammarians. We have concentrated on six areas: vocabulary,
swearing and taboo language, grammar, literacy, pronunciation,
and verbosity. Modern sociolinguistic work on sex differences in
grammar and pronunciation will be the subject of Chapters 4 and
5. Chapter 6, which looks at the general topic of communicative
competence, will include a discussion of contemporary linguistic
research on sex differences in swearing and in verbosity.

NOTES

1 The first proverb is taken from *The Oxford Dictionary of
English Proverbs*, edited by Smith and Heseltine (1935); the
second is from *Cheshire Proverbs*, collected and annotated by
Joseph C. Bridge (1917); and the last two are taken from
Jespersen (1922:253, fn.1).

2 According to Bernstein (a sociologist) restricted code is
distinguished from elaborated code in the following ways: it is
used in relatively informal situations, and speakers assume a
great deal of shared knowledge; this is reflected linguistically in
the high proportion of pronouns and tag questions, and in the
simple syntax. Linguists are not happy with the codes, and
Bernstein's claim that the ability to use them correlates with
social class is highly controversial.

3 It is reported that nursery school children in Bristol are taught a
song which goes: 'All the Daddies on the bus go read, read,
read . . . All the Mummies. on the bus go chatter, chatter,
chatter . . .' (quoted in *The Guardian*'s 'Naked Ape' column).
Primary school children in Birkenhead are taught this song
too.

Chapter Three

The historical background (II) – Anthropologists and dialectologists

3.1 INTRODUCTION

There are two major disciplines whose work touches on sex differences in language. These two disciplines – Anthropology and Dialectology – have aims and objectives which are quite distinct from those of sociolinguistics, but there are areas of overlap. Anthropologists have observed language as part of their observation of the whole spectrum of social behaviour in a given community. Dialectologists have analysed the speech of rural communities in order to investigate linguistic change and the decline of rural dialects. Both anthropologists and dialectologists have commented upon sex differences in language, and it is these comments which form the basis of this chapter.

3.2 ANTHROPOLOGISTS

Differences between the language of male and female speakers have been noted in anthropological literature since the seventeenth century. Missionaries and explorers came across societies whose linguistic behaviour caused them to speak of 'men's language' and 'women's language'. These terms overstate the case: what we find in these languages are phonological, morphological, syntactic and lexical contrasts where the sex of the speaker determines which form is chosen. I shall briefly survey some of this work to illustrate the kind of male/female variation in language that anthropologists commented on.

3.2.1 Phonological differences

The Chukchi language, spoken in Eastern Siberia, varies phonologically, depending on the sex of the speaker. Women use

/ʃ/ where men use /tʃ/ or /r/. For example, the word for *people* is pronounced /ʃamkɪʃʃɪn/ by women and /ramkɪtʃɪn/ by men.

The men and women of the Gros Ventre tribe in Montana also make consistent differences in their pronunciation (Flannery, 1946). The velar plosive /k/ is replaced by an affricate in the men's speech, so where the women say /wakinsihiθa/ (newborn child), the men say /wadʒinsihiθa/. The word for bread is pronounced /kja'tsa/ by the women, and /dʒa'tsa/ by the men. In this community, pronunciation is a defining marker of sexual identity: if anyone uses the wrong form, they are considered to be bisexual by older members of the tribe. Flannery hypothesises that fear of being laughed at for such errors has helped to erode the use of the language by the younger generation, who tend to speak English.

3.2.2 Morphological differences

Edward Sapir (1929, quoted in Yaguello 1978) describes a language spoken by the Yana (in California) where the language used between men differs morphologically from that used in other situations (men to women, women to men, women to women). The words used in this men-to-men variety are longer than those used in the communal language. It seems that in a minority of cases the men add a suffix to the primary form, following a rule which can roughly be stated as follows: *When a word in the communal language ends with a long vowel, a diphthong or a consonant, or if the word is a monosyllable, the men's language adds a suffix /-na/*, e.g. /ba/ (stag) → /bana/; /au/ (fire) → /auna/. In the majority of cases the form in the communal language appears to be a logical *abbreviation* of the male form, following a rule which can roughly be stated as follows: *When a word in the men's language ends in a short vowel – /a, i, u/ – this vowel is lost and the preceding consonant becomes voiceless; thus /b, d, g, dʒ/ + short vowel → /p', t', k', tʃ'/*, e.g. /gagi/ (crow) → /gak'/; /p'adza/ (snow) → /p'atʃ'/.

This second rule can be accounted for by the principle of morphophonemic economy (there is a tendency in all languages for words to get simplified – cf *omnibus* → *bus, refrigerator* → *fridge*, etc.). In other words, the men's language seems to preserve historically older forms. Sapir suggests that the reduced female forms symbolise women's lower status: the men's fuller forms are associated with ceremony and formality. This is an interesting case of male speech being associated with conservatism and linguistic purity, characteristics now conventionally associated with women's language (this will be discussed at greater length in Chapters 4 and 8).

Among the Koasati, a Muskogean Indian tribe in Louisiana,

certain forms of the verb vary according to the sex of the speaker (Haas 1944). For example, where the women's form ends in a nasalised vowel, the men's form ends in -*s*. The following are examples:

Women	Men	
lakawtakkǫ́	*lakawtakkós*	I am not lifting it
lakawwą́	*lakawwá.s*	he will lift it
ká.	*ká.s*	he is saying

Where the women's form has the falling pitch-stress on its final syllable and ends in a short vowel followed by /l/, the men's form involves high pitch-stress and replaces /l/ with /s/.

Women	Men	
lakawwîl	*lakawwîs*	I am lifting it
molhîl	*molhís*	we are peeling it
lakawhôl	*lakawhós*	lift it! (to 2nd person plural)

In this community, it is the women's language which is conservative and which represents an earlier stage in the language. In 1944, Haas found that only the older women were maintaining the distinction; the younger women used the men's forms. The women's forms are presumably obsolete now.

3.2.3 Lexical differences

Sex differences in vocabulary were frequently reported by early anthropologists. We will look at two examples here; two other examples are given in the next section (3.3).

In most languages, the pronoun system marks sex distinctions in the third person (e.g. *he/she*), but the distinction is less commonly made in the first and second persons where sex of speaker is involved. Japanese is a language which marks sex in all three persons of the pronoun (Bodine 1975a). There is a first person form *watakushi* which can be used by either male or female speakers, but male speakers tend to use *boku* and women *atashi* (an abbreviated form of *watakushi*). There are two second person pronouns: *anata*, which can be used to male or female addressees, and *kimi*, a form used exclusively by men when addressing men or women of equal or inferior rank.

In his work on the Trobriand islanders, Malinowski (1929, quoted in Yaguello 1978) established that their kinship terminology is organised on the basis of two criteria:

1. same/different sex;
2. older/younger.

This means that the word for *sister*, for example, will vary depending on the sex of the speaker, and according to whether the speaker is older or younger than the sibling. The diagram below (Fig. 3.1) shows how the system works for the relationships of brother, sister, brother-in-law and sister-in-law.

Figure 3.1: Trobriand islanders' terms for sister, brother, sister-in-law, brother-in-law (based on Yaguello 1978:27)

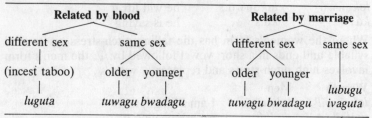

In the case of the relationship we call *sister*, the Trobrianders have three terms (*luguta*, *tuwagu*, *bwadagu*) for our one. Conversely, they make no distinction between a man's sister and a woman's brother (both are *luguta*), nor between a man's brother and a woman's sister if the age difference is the same in both cases (*tuwagu* or *bwadagu*).

We can see why earlier scholars were misled into talking of men's and women's languages. In particular, where English and other European languages distinguish kin on the basis of **sex of the spoken about**, the Trobriand language, like Chiquito, Yana, and many others, distinguishes kinship terms on the basis of **sex of speaker**. This means that Trobriand islanders give different names to relationships we see as 'the same', but only one name to relationships we perceive as 'different'.

3.3 ANTHROPOLOGICAL EXPLANATIONS

It is clear that none of these examples constitutes a case of separate languages for women and men. Observers mistakenly described the phenomena they came across in terms of separate male/female languages as a result of both linguistic naïvety and a tendency to exaggerate. Their hypotheses about the origins of sex differences in language were inevitably skewed by their belief in polarised sex varieties. The two main explanatory factors put forward by anthropologists were **taboo** and **contact with speakers of other languages**.

Taboo operates in all societies, proscribing certain forms of behaviour, including linguistic behaviour. In British society today, topics of conversation such as excretion or sexual activity are taboo in most contexts. In so-called 'primitive' societies, what is or is not permitted is stringently controlled socially. Taboos are part of the structure which maintains social order.

A good example of taboo and its effects on language is reported by Caroline Humphrey in an article on women and taboo (Humphrey 1978). She investigated what constituted incorrect or improper behaviour for women in Mongolia. Most linguistic taboos in Mongolia are concerned with *names*. Mongols avoid using the names of dead people, predatory animals and certain mountains and rivers thought to be inhabited by spirits. More particularly, women are absolutely forbidden to use the names of their husband's older brothers, father, father's brothers or grandfather. This taboo extends beyond the names of the husband's male relatives: women are not allowed to use *any word or syllable* which is the same as, or sounds like, any of the forbidden names. For example, where the name *Shar* is taboo, the woman must not use either the name or the word *shar* (=yellow), but has to substitute *angir*, a word which refers to a yellow-coloured duck. Or if the tabooed name is *Xarzuu* (derived from *xarax* = to look at), the woman must also avoid the word *xar* (=black) and has to use instead *bargaan*, which means 'darkish or obscure'. It is not surprising that earlier reports talked of 'women's language' among the Mongols. However, such taboos only affect vocabulary; other aspects of language are unaffected. Moreover, each woman affected by such a taboo will have different linguistic problems, depending on the names of her male relatives-by-marriage. So while it can result in distinct female vocabularies, taboo as a social force is hardly sufficient explanation of the other sex differences which occur in language.

Contact with speakers of other languages occurs when there is an invasion, or when men marry women from outside their village or tribe (as is the custom in some societies). The most well-known case of linguistic sex differences said to result from the marrying of people speaking different languages is that of the Carib Indians. In his account of the people of lesser Antilles, written in 1665, Rochefort claimed that the men and women spoke different languages:

> The savage natives of Dominica say that the reason for this is that when the Caribs came to occupy the islands, these were inhabited by an Arawak tribe which they exterminated completely, with the exception of the women, whom they married in order to populate the country. Now, these women kept their own language and taught it to their daughters . . . It is asserted that there is some similarity between the speech of the continental Arawaks and that of the Carib women.
> (as quoted in Jespersen 1922:237)

It is clear from other evidence that this is another case of separate lexical items for women and men in certain areas; it is not a case of two separate languages. Moreover, the invasion theory is not totally convincing, especially as the linguistic variation found among Carib Indians is similar to that found in other American Indian groups (Trudgill 1974b:86). Contact with speakers of other languages will not do as an explanation for sex differences in language in general, since such differences occur in all known languages.

3.4 SOME PROBLEMS WITH ANTHROPOLOGICAL WORK ON SEX DIFFERENCES

The major defect of anthropological work is that anthropologists failed to see that sex differences in language were not exclusively a feature of 'primitive' people and of distant exotic cultures. It is reasonable to ask the question: Why did they ignore sex differences in the European languages they were familiar with? The answer seems to be that they defined the problem in terms of **sex-exclusive** differences. That is, they commented on differences between women's and men's usage where certain linguistic forms were reserved exclusively for the use of one sex or the other. All the examples quoted so far in this chapter are of this kind. The variation in male/female language found in European languages, however, involves **sex-preferential** differences, that is, while women's and men's language differs, there are no forms associated exclusively with one sex; rather there is a tendency for women or men to prefer a certain form. For example, as we shall see in the following chapters, women in Britain tend to use forms closer to Standard English, while men tend to use a higher proportion of non-standard forms. The difference between sex-exclusive and sex-preferential usage seems to be a reflection of the difference between pre-literate, non-industrialised societies and literate, highly industrialised societies; the former tend to have clearly segregated sex roles, unlike modern European societies where sex roles are much less rigidly structured.

Despite their failure to generalise their discoveries to more familiar societies, anthropologists at least drew attention to the way in which human societies use sex as a salient social category, and to the linguistic differences which arise directly from this social structure. More recently, anthropology has had an important influence on the developing discipline of sociolinguistics. In general terms, the anthropologists' insistence on the significance of cultural context has underpinned the sociolinguist's conviction that the study of the ideal speaker/hearer in a homogeneous speech community is too narrow a field. More particularly, sociolinguistic methodology has borrowed directly from anthropological field techniques; the study of groups as working wholes and the concept of the social network as a tool of analysis are leading to exciting new developments in sociolinguistic research. Such research will be described in detail in Chapter 6.

3.5 DIALECTOLOGISTS

Dialectologists, unlike anthropologists, have always been sensitive to sex differences in their own (that is, European) languages. Ironically, this has resulted in our having virtually no data on such differences, for reasons which will become apparent during the following discussion. We shall discuss the work of dialectologists as it relates to sex differences under three headings: women as informants, the questionnaire, and the fieldworker.

3.5.1 Women as informants

The choice of informants is of crucial importance in any linguistic survey. Since the Holy Grail of traditional dialectology was 'pure' dialect, which had to be recorded before it died out, dialectologists chose as informants those who, in their view, spoke 'pure' dialect. The circularity of this procedure was uncritically accepted. Their methodology contrasts markedly with that of modern sociolinguistic surveys, which have adopted the methods of the social sciences, taking a representative sample of informants chosen randomly from the electoral roll, or some equivalent list. Because dialectologists' choice of informants was so unrepresentative, we have little idea what sort of linguistic variation existed in the rural communities studied. Certain members of the community were included; others were excluded. We have no comparative data to confirm or refute the dialectologists' claim that some members of the speech community spoke a more 'pure' form of the dialect than others.

Who did dialectologists choose as informants? The answer to this question reveals that their choice depended largely on folklinguistic beliefs. Dialectologists favoured older members of the community as informants (for obvious, if not scientific reasons), but they disagreed about the merits of female as opposed to male informants. One view was that women were the best informants because of their innate conservatism. This view was expressed by a great variety of dialectologists, from the end of the nineteenth century up to the 1940s, in areas as different as Slovene, Switzerland, Flanders and Romania. The general view is that stated by Wartburg in his review of Griera's Linguistic Atlas of Catalonia (which is criticised for its lack of women informants):

> Everyone knows that as far as language is concerned women are more conservative than men; they conserve the speech of our forbears more faithfully.[1]
> (Wartburg 1925:113).

This view is supported by the following 'reasons':

1. Women hardly ever leave their village, unlike men;
2. Women stay at home and talk ('chat') to each other, and don't mix with strangers;
3. Women don't do military service.

The opposite view – that women are *not* conservative – was held by many other dialectologists, including the hugely influential Gilliéron, director of the linguistic survey of France (the first major survey to use a trained fieldworker). These dialectologists preferred *men* as informants, since they considered men's speech to be closer to the 'pure' dialect. The general view is clearly stated by Harold Orton in his *Introduction to the Survey of English Dialects*:

> In this country men speak vernacular more frequently, more consistently, and more genuinely than women.
> (Orton 1962:15)

The innovative nature of women's speech is stressed:

> Women's speech is not conservative. Women, who are usually said to be more conservative than men, accept new words quite readily.[2]
> (from Pop's account of Gilliéron 1880)

Unlike those who believe in women's conservatism, these dialectologists offer us no explanations. Gauchat, for example, tells us that women are more innovative and then describes their lives as follows:

> They spend much more time in the home, with other people, cooking and washing, and talking more than men, who are busy with their agricultural work; you see the men at their work, silent and often on their own for the whole day.[3]

We are presumably meant to infer from the different life styles of the two sexes a reason for their differing linguistic usage. But this description does not explain why women should be more innovative than men. In fact, the female way of life described here is virtually identical to that described by dialectologists in the 'women are conservative' camp. As far as we can see any difference, it is in the way the *men*'s lives are described: the

42

dialectologists in the first group stress the men's interaction with strangers, travel, military service; while those in the second group either don't describe the men's lives, or portray them as isolated.

The explanation which seems to underlie the second group of studies is women's supposed sensitivity to linguistic norms. It is assumed that standard norms will have more influence on women's speech than on men's; women, who have little status in society, seek to acquire status through their use of language. Stanley Ellis, chief fieldworker for the Survey of English Dialects, comments:

> Women were always seen as a refining and "improving" influence. It was suggested that this often came about because young country girls used to have a spell as indoor servants in better class homes and came under the influence of better speech.

(Ellis, personal communication)

The concepts of both conservatism and status-consciousness on the part of women are introduced into dialect studies in a somewhat *ad hoc* manner, depending on how women's speech is perceived. Neither seems a very satisfactory explanation of linguistic sex differences. (For a fuller critique of conservatism and status-consciousness as explanatory factors, see Cameron & Coates 1985.)

The evidence suggests, then, that attitudes to informants were preconceived and highly subjective. Not surprisingly, we find contradictions: Gilliéron, whose survey covered the whole of France, argued that women were not conservative linguistically, while Meunier, in his much smaller study of the Nivernais region of France, favoured women as informants because of their conservatism; Jaberg and Jud, in their major dialect survey of Italy and Southern Switzerland, also assume the linguistic conservatism of women, but one of their fieldworkers (Rohlfs) is quoted as saying 'the pronunciation of vowels by women doesn't differ only from that of men – who possess vowels which are purer and clearer – but from area to area . . .'[4] (Jaberg 1936:21 n 3). Rohlfs definitely seems to be claiming that men's pronunciation of vowels was 'purer' than women's. Pop, in his comprehensive account of dialect study (Pop 1950), can hardly fail to notice such discrepancies. He is basically an adherent of the 'women are conservative' camp, but he advocates a detailed comparative study of the pronunciation of men and women, since, he says, 'it certainly seems, although people often assert the contrary, that women's language displays more innovations than men's in certain cases'[5] (Pop, 1950:195).

Only one dialectologist, out of all those I have surveyed, states specifically that he is *not* aware of sex differences in the speech community he is studying. This is Angus McIntosh, director of the Survey of Scottish dialects. He writes: 'As to sex, there is no evidence which shows conclusively whether men or women make better informants in Scotland' (McIntosh 1952:90).

So who did the dialectologists choose as informants? On the basis of their published views, we would expect the first group to select women (since they describe women as linguistically conservative) and the second to select men (since they describe men as using the vernacular more than women). In fact, with the exception of the German–Swiss survey and McIntosh's Scottish survey (in both of which the fieldworkers interviewed one man and one woman in each locality), *all* the dialect surveys for which I have figures favoured men. The following Table (3.1) gives details.

As this Table shows, women were very poorly represented in

Table 3.1: Table to show proportion of women informants in dialect surveys (source: Pop 1950)

Dialect survey	Date of publication	Male informants	Female informants	Total informants	% women
France (Gillieron)	1902–10	640	60*	700*	8.57
Catalonia (Griera)	1923–39	107	1	108	0.93
S. Austria (Tesniere)	1925	70	18	88	20.45
Italy/Switz. (Jaberg & Jud)	1928–40	380	40*	420*	9.52
Sardinia (Pellis)	1933–35	55	5	60	8.33
Corsica (Bottiglioni)	1933–42	61	6	67	8.96
Italy (Bartoli)	1933	316	48	364	13.19
Belg. Congo (De Boeck)	1942	?	0	?	0.00
North China (Giet)	1946	495	29	524	5.53
England (Orton)	1962–78	867	122	989	12.34

(* = approximate figure)

dialect surveys. Moreover, a detailed examination of dialect survey findings shows that the few female informants are not spread evenly. The Survey of English Dialects, for example, investigated the 39 counties of England, but this does not mean that 12 per cent of informants in each county were women, as we would expect (see Table 3.1); in fact, in 7 counties, *no* women were interviewed (Worcestershire, Gloucestershire, Northamptonshire, Huntingdonshire, Cambridgeshire, Wiltshire, Devon).

When we look for explanations for this uneven pattern of sampling, we find that dialectologists express reservations about women as informants. Even dialectologists who see women as better informants on *linguistic* grounds (because of their supposed conservatism) reject them for non-linguistic reasons. For example, women are said to be too busy or too timid, or embarrassed at being asked to speak patois in front of a researcher. A typical 'explanation' for failing to interview more women is that of Sever Pop, who was Director of the dialect survey of Romania:

> The investigator comes up against problems in persuading women to give up two or three days to the project, since household chores prevent them from doing so, and they feel embarrassed at sitting down at the table with a 'city gentleman'.[6]
> (Pop 1950:725)

Pop at least adduces reasons which seem relevant to the fieldworker's task. Other dialectologists, however, explain their omission of women on blatantly sexist grounds. The following is taken from an article by Griera, a Catholic priest who was responsible for the Linguistic Atlas of Catalonia:

> The reasons for my doing so [*i.e. excluding women*] are: the impossibility of their maintaining attention during a long questionnaire lasting several days; the fact that their knowledge of objects is, in general, more limited than men's, and, above all, their lack of firm concepts which is reflected in imprecise naming of objects.
> (Griera 1928)[7]

Even though dialectologists are aware that they tend to favour men as informants, it seems probable, to judge from the following comment of an expert fieldworker, that they had no idea *how few* women were actually involved as informants: 'The informants I used during my spell as fieldworker for The Survey of English Dialects in the 1950s were far more men than women. I would estimate about one informant in four or five were [*sic*] female' (Ellis, personal communication). As we can see from Table 3.1, fewer than one informant in eight was female.

There are two aspects of dialect study which may help us to

explain the predominance of men as informants. These are the questionnaire, which was traditionally used to structure the interview, to guarantee comparability, and to ensure that the desired responses were obtained from every informant; and the fieldworker, usually a trained scholar who was sent out into a given area by the director of the survey, to conduct interviews with informants.

3.5.2   The questionnaire

The questionnaire, 'the central instrument used in the systematic collection of dialect' (Francis 1983:52), may seem an innocent tool of research, but besides determining in advance what linguistic items are to be scrutinised, it predetermines in other ways what is to be included and what not.

Most questionnaires, both those in postal surveys and those employing fieldworkers, were divided into sections, and some of these sections would be aimed specifically at women, and some at men. The German-Swiss Linguistic Atlas based its choice of informants on this division: 'The responses for the dialect of each locality were given by a man and a woman of the district: the man replied to the questions concerning men's work; the women to those concerning feminine occupations'[8] (Pop 1950:770). The German-Swiss survey was unusual in interviewing as many women as men, but we should note the rigid segregation of questions into those for women and those for men. This presumably reflects the dialectologist's concern with **lexicon**. Traditional dialectology aimed to establish 'what a three-legged milking stool is called in several hundred different places' (McIntosh 1952:70). Many dialectologists assumed that men's and women's vocabularies differed as a reflection of their social roles. As McIntosh comments:

> Experience has shown that a conventional portmanteau questionnaire cannot be filled in completely with the help of only one person; the housewife lets one down on agricultural terms, the farmer on kitchen terms, and often some local expert has to be hunted out specially to deal with such items as flowers or birds. (McIntosh 1952:89)

We will look at two examples of dialect study to show how the structure of the questionnaire affected the choice of informant.

1. Navarro, who was responsible for the Linguistic Atlas of Puerto Rico, is reported as justifying his virtual exclusion of women informants on the grounds that they wouldn't know the replies to his questions:
   Since the questionnaire was designed to find out in particular

about agricultural terminology, women could not give good replies. For this reason there are only two women among the informants.[9]
(Pop 1950:452)

2. Wirth, director of the Linguistic Atlas of Sorabe (a Western Slav dialect), was particularly interested in domestic vocabulary. As Pop says:
   'Since his questionnaire was principally concerned with the terminology of the dwelling place and housework, he was obliged to appeal to women to collaborate.'[10]
   (Pop 1950:981)

Table 3.2 (over the page) gives details of the thirty-one sections included in the questionnaire for the *Atlas linguistique et ethnographique du Lyonnais* (Gardette 1968). This is one of the more recent regional atlases produced by French dialectologists, yet the built-in assumption of male-as-norm is still there: of the thirty-one sections, two (nos 20 and 21) are specifically marked as 'Women's Life'. Women's life has to be marked because it is taken for granted that the majority of sections will relate to men.

We can see from the preceding discussion that one of the reasons women were not used as informants was that (male) dialectologists defined which areas of life and therefore which lexical sets were worthy of study from an essentially androcentric viewpoint.

It is especially common for the interviewer to shift to a woman – often the wife of a principal male informant – for those parts of the questionnaire which deal with the house, the kitchen, the children, and other areas commonly considered to be women's province.
(Francis 1983:86)

Since men's work was regarded as of prime interest, women's work, and therefore women's vocabulary, was normally regarded as peripheral. Since dialectologists were also interested in phonology and grammar, this concentration on male language does not seem defensible. There are indications, however, that women may have been involved more than at first appears. The description of the principal informant at point number 2 for the Dialect Atlas of SubCarpathian Poland (published in 1934) tells us that he was called Jean Klamerus, that he was 75 years old, that he was rather deaf and slow. He was interviewed in the presence of his daughter-in-law, who is described as an energetic, intelligent woman, a good informant from a grammatical point of view, and very good from a phonetic and lexicological point of view. Pop comments that it was the daughter-in-law who replied to most of

Table 3.2: Questionnaire for *Atlas linguistique et ethnographique du Lyonnais* (Francis 1983:60)

Section	Number of questions
1. Meadow, hay, rake, fork	57
2. Grain, sowing, harvest	58
3. Threshing, the flail	57
4. Yoke, goad	39
5. Plows and working the land	55
6. Carts and wagons	66
7. The vineyard	89
8. The wood	54
9. The garden, potatoes, root vegetables	36
10. Cattle, horses, donkeys	63
11. Sheep, goats, swine	62
12. The barnyard	50
13. The barnyard (concluded), bees, dog, cat	43
14. Milk, butter, cheese	64
15. Bread	43
16. Trees (other than fruit-trees)	59
17. Fruit-trees	59
18. Birds, flies, parasites	58
19. Harmful animals, snakes, water creatures, insects	48
20. Women's life: 1. the bed, housekeeping, meals	59
21. Women's life: 2. washing, sewing	52
22. The house: 1. generalities, doors and windows, kitchen	61
23. The house: 2. lamps, fireplace, bedroom, outbuildings	56
24. Weather: winds, rain, snow, sun	70
25. The stars, landscape	45
26. The calendar	44
27. The day, kinship	48
28. From cradle to grave	107
29. The body	85
30. Clothing; manure; occupations	50
31. Hemp	31
Total lexical items	1,875
Morphological items	68

the questions[11] (Pop 1952). How often a female relative gave the responses which are credited to a man, we cannot tell.

3.5.3 The fieldworker

Another reason why men were chosen as informants rather than women was probably that the vast majority of fieldworkers were themselves men. This is so much the normal pattern that McIntosh defines the fieldworker as 'a man [*sic*] specially trained to listen to peculiarities of speech' (McIntosh 1952:66). The first women fieldworkers were those involved in the Linguistic Atlas of New England (2 women out of 10 fieldworkers) and the Survey of English Dialects (2 women out of 11 fieldworkers).

If we imagine Edmont Edmont, fieldworker for the French Linguistic Atlas, arriving on his bicycle at one of the 639 localities he surveyed between 1896 and 1900, it seems plausible to argue that he was far more likely to get into conversation with, and subsequently to interview, other men. Edmont did in fact interview only about 60 women out of his 700 informants. Kurath, director of the New England survey, writes the following in his section on choosing informants:

> After some experience in the field, he [*the fieldworker*] may discover that informal contacts in the general store, barber shop or local tavern can provide him with useful leads.
> (Kurath 1972:13)

(Note the use of *he/him* in this extract.) This is the advice of an eminent dialectologist to others in the field after a century of dialect study: presumably it reflects traditional practice. If the norm was male fieldworkers making contact with potential informants in the male setting of the barber shop or the tavern, then it is hardly surprising that women were rarely interviewed.

If we look at what happened when the fieldworker was *female*, we can test the hypothesis that the sex of the fieldworker influenced the selection of informants. An examination of those sections of the Survey of English Dialects where a woman was the fieldworker shows a significant increase in the number of women interviewed. As Table 3.1 shows, for the survey as a whole, 12 per cent of informants were women. For Leicestershire and Rutland, the two counties wholly investigated by a woman fieldworker, the figures are 33 per cent and 40 per cent respectively.

The sex of the fieldworker should be taken into account for other reasons too. Only recently have linguists become fully aware of the effect an interviewer can have on an informant's language. Labov has demonstrated convincingly that by replacing a white middle-class interviewer with a younger, black interviewer (and also by reducing the formality of the situation by sitting on the floor, eating crisps, etc.), the black child who was previously thought to have virtually no language can be shown to be a fluent speaker (Labov 1969). It seems highly probable that women feel constrained in the presence of a male interviewer (see Pop's comment quoted above, p. 45), and will therefore produce more formal language. This may help to explain the experience of Orton and others that women's speech was closer to standard norms. (However, modern sociolinguistic surveys, carried out by both women and men, are still finding that in Britain women's speech is closer to standard, as we shall see in Chapter 4.)

In more recent dialect surveys, despite the growth of sociolinguistic research and methodology, the presence of women as fieldworkers is still a matter for comment. The following is an extract from Gardette's discussion of methodology in his *Atlas linguistique et ethnographique du Lyonnais*:

> The four female fieldworkers of our team had in general as good results as those of Monsieur Girodet and myself. Those who interviewed in areas where they were known, among informants who claimed common friends, often received a particularly sympathetic welcome.
> (Gardette 1968:44)

This shows an understanding that the relationship between fieldworker and informant is one which can vary. But it is also patronising, since it is surely gratuitous to comment on the women's results being as good as those of the two male fieldworkers. In a discussion of women as fieldworkers, Francis argues that women may not be ideal, since male informants may not want to respond frankly in their presence. I shall quote this passage in full as it is very revealing of attitudes in dialectology:

> It has been pointed out that women [*as fieldworkers*] do have one disadvantage: the kind of old-fashioned rustic who constituted the usual informant in traditional surveys is likely to be squeamish about discussing some topics and using some lexical items considered to be improper in the presence of a woman. This is true, but such items constitute a very small part of most questionnaires. On the other side it may be said that a woman fieldworker may have much better success than a man in eliciting some of the special vocabulary of women from female informants.
> (Francis 1983:84)

Note how the writer doesn't feel any need to make explicit the fact that the 'old-fashioned rustic who constituted the usual informant' is obviously male. Just as women are often only included as informants for the sake of special 'women's vocabulary', so women fieldworkers become accepted since they may be better at eliciting this 'women's' language.

3.6 CONCLUSION

It is now seen as a major weakness of traditional dialectology that it selected informants on such an unscientific basis. Because of assumptions made by fieldworkers and their directors about male/female differences in language, women have been largely ignored in dialect studies. Where they have been included, it has been to supplement the fieldworker's information, rather than as full members of the speech community. Dialectology, in other words, has marginalised women speakers. Traditional dialectologists defined the true vernacular in terms of male informants, and organised their questionnaires around what was seen as the man's world.

A desire to improve on the methodology of dialect surveys, combined with a growing interest in *urban* dialects, gave impetus to the growth of sociolinguistics. Sociolinguists, like dialectologists, are interested in variation in language and in the phonology, grammar and lexicon of non-standard varieties. But where dialectologists focused on the *spatial* dimension, studying regional variation, sociolinguists have shifted attention to the *social* dimension and study variation due to factors such as age, sex, social class, education, ethnic group. Dialectologists tended to ignore the speech of women, for all sorts of conscious and unconscious reasons: some dialectologists claimed that women's speech was more standard than men's and therefore less interesting for their research; others, as we have seen, saw women as more conservative linguistically. We have no hard evidence that women's speech was more or less standard, more or less vernacular than men's. If dialectologists had sampled populations in the way sociolinguists do, by interviewing a representative cross-sample, then we might have had some very interesting data on linguistic sex differences. As it is, we have, as the end-product of most dialect surveys, a record of the language of non-mobile, older, rural *men*, and we don't know whether women's language differed significantly from theirs or not.

It is only with the advent of quantitative sociolinguistic studies that we have reliable data on sex differences in language. Quantitative sociolinguistic studies which explore sex differences in language will be described in the two following chapters.

NOTES

1 'Tout le monde sait qu'en matière de langage les femmes sont plus conservatrices que les hommes, qu'elles conservent plus

fidèlement le parler des aieux' (Wartburg 1925:113, as quoted in Pop 1950:373).

2 'Le parler des femmes n'est pas conservateur. Les femmes, que d'ordinaire on affirme être plus conservatrices que les hommes, acceptent assez facilement les mots nouveaux' (Pop's account of Gilliéron *Patois de la commune de Vionnaz* (*Bas Valais*) (1880), Pop 1950:180).

3 '[les femmes] passent beaucoup plus de temps à la maison, en société, à cuisiner, à laver et qui parlent plus que les hommes, pris par les travaux de la campagne, au milieu desquels on les voit taciturnes, et souvent isolés toute la journee' (Pop's account of Gauchat *L'unité phonetique dans le patois d'une commune* (1905), Pop 1950:194).

4 'La prononciation des voyelles chez la population feminine ne diffère pas seulement de celle des hommes – qui possèdent des voyelles plus pures et plus claires – mais de quartier à quartier et quelquefois même d'individu à individu' (K. Jaberg *Aspects géographiques du langage*, 1936, as quoted in Pop 1950:579).

5 ' . . .il semble bien, quoique l'on affirme souvent le contraire, que le langage des femmes présente dans certains cas plus d'innovations que celui des hommes' (Pop 1950:195).

6 'L'enquêteur rencontre des difficultés à persuader les femmes de sacrifier deux ou trois jours pour l'enquête, car les soins du ménage les en empêchent, et elles se trouvent gênées de s'attabler avec "un monsieur de la ville".' (Pop 1950:725).

7 'Les raons que m'hi obligaren son: l'impossibilitat de guardar atencio durant un llarg interrogatori d'alguns dies; el tenir els coneixements de les coses, generalment, mes limitats que els homes i, sobretot, la falta de fixesa s'idees que es tradeix en una denominacio imprecisa de les coses' (A.Griera *Entom de l'Atlas linguistique de l'Italie et de la Suisse Meridionale*, 1928, as quoted in Pop 1950:373). I am grateful to Max Wheeler for translating this extract.

8 'Les réponses pour le parler de chaque localité ont été données par *un homme et par une femme du pays*: le premier répondait aux demandes concernant les travaux faits par les hommes; la seconde à celles touchant les occupations feminines' (Pop 1950:770).

9 'La questionnaire ayant ete redigé en vue de connaître surtout la terminologie agricole, les femmes ne pouvaient pas donner de bonnes réponses. Pour cette raison, il n'y a que deux femmes parmi les informateurs' (Pop's account of Navarro's

fieldwork for the *Linguistic Atlas of Puerto Rico*, 1948, in Pop
1950:432).

10 'Son questionnaire regardant en premier lieu la terminologie
de l'habitation et du ménage l'obligeait d'ailleurs à faire appel
à la collaboration des femmes' (Pop 1950:981).

11 '. . . c'est plutôt elle [i.e. the daughter-in-law] qui a donné
les réponses' (Pop 1950:977).

Part Two

The Sociolinguistic Evidence

Chapter Four

Quantitative studies

4.1 INTRODUCTION

In this chapter, we shall look at sex differences in language revealed by quantitative sociolinguistic studies. The chapter begins with a brief description of classic sociolinguistic work, with its analysis of linguistic variation in relation to social class of speaker and speech style (formal or informal). The central section will examine in some detail four examples of sociolinguistic work done in Britain which reveal significant sex differences. The chapter ends with a discussion of the reasons underlying this kind of sociolinguistic variation.

4.2 THE STANDARD PARADIGM

Classic sociolinguistic research, such as William Labov's in New York and Peter Trudgill's in Norwich, aimed to examine the correlation between linguistic variation and other variables, in particular social class. These quantitative studies revealed clear social stratification, and gave rise to the related concepts of **prestige** and **stigma**. **Prestige** is said to be attached to those linguistic forms normally used by the social group with the most social status. The process of standardisation almost always leads to the development of notions of correctness; members of a given speech community will come to acknowledge that one particular variety – the standard dialect – is more 'correct' than other varieties. Correct usage will be seen as being enshrined in this variety, which will accordingly have high prestige. The use of the standard variety in the major institutions of society – the law, education, broadcasting – perpetuates this prestige. Conversely, **stigma** is attached to non-standard forms. This stigma may be overt, as in the case of forms which are the subject of heated condemnation on newspaper correspondence pages, or which are frowned on in school[1] (e.g. 'dropping' initial /h/, *ain't, disinterested* for *uninterested*); or it may be beneath the level of public consciousness, as in the case of many of the forms investigated by sociolinguists. As interest in the use and persistence of non-standard forms has grown, non-standard varieties have come to be known as the **vernacular**.

Another important concept employed in quantitative sociolinguistic studies is that of the **linguistic variable**. A variable, to put it simply, is something which varies in a socially significant way. A linguistic variable then, is a linguistic unit with various realisations: these are called **variants**. The phoneme /t/ is a linguistic variable in contemporary English: when it occurs intervocalically (between vowels) in words like *butter* or phrases like *bit of*, it has two variants, the voiceless alveolar plosive [t] and the glottal stop [ʔ]. In other words, depending on circumstances, *bit of* may be realised as [bɪtəv] or [bɪʔəv]. Linguistic variables can be phonological (like /t/ in the example) or grammatical or lexical. Not all linguistic units are variables, of course.

Sociolinguists are interested in linguistic variables because they don't vary randomly – they vary systematically in relation to other variables, such as social class, age and sex. In other words, linguistic variables are involved in **co-variation** with other variables. Londoners who say [bæʔə] for *butter* will still be referring to a substance made from cream which we spread on bread, but they will be revealing something of their social/regional origins in choosing that particular variant. Speakers' use of linguistic variables is one of the ways in which they locate themselves in social space. Linguistic variables, in other words, are linguistically equivalent but socially different ways of saying the same thing.

4.2.1 Social stratification

The classic pattern of social stratification revealed by quantitative studies is shown in diagrammatic form below (Fig. 4.1). The vertical axis represents group score (measured as the average of the scores of all the individuals in that group and converted to a percentage figure); a score of 100 per cent represents consistent use of the prestige form. The horizontal axis represents the degree of formality in the speech situation. Notice the following three points:

1. each social class group uses a higher proportion of prestige forms (has a higher score) in formal speech, and a lower proportion of prestige forms (a lower

score) in informal speech – this produces the sloping lines;

2. in any given speech style (i.e. at any point on the horizontal axis from least formal to most formal) social class stratification is maintained: each group maintains its position relative to other groups – this produces the parallel, non-overlapping lines in the diagram;

3. use of the imaginary linguistic variable plotted here varies from 100 to 0 per cent: the prestige variant is used consistently by the upper middle class in the most formal contexts, but it is not used at all by the lower working class in the least formal contexts (such consistent use of non-standard forms in non-formal contexts is what many sociolinguistics are now trying to observe, in order to arrive at accurate descriptions of the vernacular).

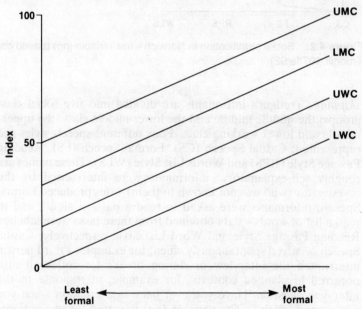

Figure 4.1: A diagrammatic representation of social stratification

As you might expect, representations of social stratification as it is actually found in modern urban communities are not as tidy as Fig. 4.1. Figure 4.2 below is adapted from Peter Trudgill's Norwich survey (Trudgill 1974a), and shows the relative scores for the variable (ng), as found at the ends of words like *hopping*,

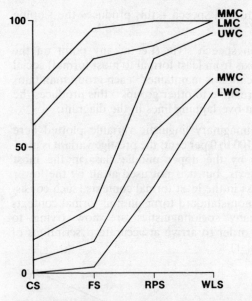

Figure 4.2: Social stratification in Norwich – the variable (ng) (based on Trudgill 1974a:92)

skipping. Trudgill's informants are divided into five social class groups: the middle middle and the lower middle class, the upper, middle and lower working class. Four different speech styles are represented: Casual Speech (CS), Formal Speech (FS), Reading Passage Style (RPS) and Words List Style (WLS). These names are roughly self-explanatory: informants were interviewed by the investigator (who was not known to them) – this produced Formal Speech; informants were asked to read a passage aloud, and to read a list of words – data obtained from these tasks were labelled Reading Passage Style and Word List Style respectively; Casual Speech occurred spontaneously when, for example, a third person interrupted the interview or during breaks for coffee; it also occurred in planned contexts, for example, in response to the interview question 'Have you ever been in a situation when you had a good laugh?'. The variable (ng) is scored for two variants only. A score of 100 per cent represents consistent RP pronunciation: [ŋ], while a score of 0 per cent represents consistent non-standard pronunciation: [n].

Here you can see that, although the five lines do not slope evenly (as in the idealised diagram), they all rise from left to right; in other words, all five social class groups in Norwich use the prestige variant [ŋ] more in more formal speech styles. And while the lines are not equidistant from each other, they do not cross over each other; in other words, social stratification is maintained in all the four speech styles investigated. Note the difference between the three working class groups and the two middle class groups in the two less formal speech styles: there is a noticeable gap between the two sets of lines at the left hand side of the diagram. Scores range from 0 per cent (the lower working class in Casual Speech) to 100 per cent (the two middle-class groups in Word List Style). Figure 4.2 demonstrates the range of social class and stylistic variation which (ng) is involved in in Norwich.

The complex but regular pattern exhibited here by (ng), and represented in idealised form in Fig. 4.1, is thought to be typical of a linguistic variable with stable social significance, that is, a linguistic variable not involved in change.

4.2.2 Linguistic variables undergoing change

The other classic pattern revealed by quantitative sociolinguistic research is typical of a linguistic variable undergoing change. An idealised diagram is given in Fig. 4.3. Note that both social stratification and the slope up from left to right are maintained. The main difference between Fig. 4.3 and the diagram for a

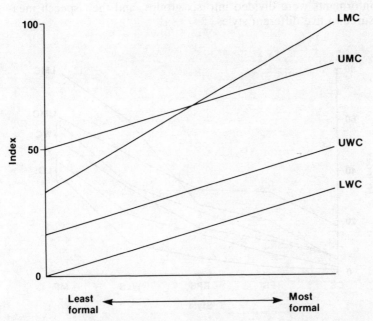

Figure 4.3: A diagrammatic representation of a linguistic variable undergoing change

stable linguistic variable (Fig. 4.1) is the **crossover** pattern which Fig. 4.3 shows. The lower middle class (the second highest status group) shows a much greater shift towards the prestige form in formal styles than any other social group – note the steepness of the slope – so great in fact that it has a higher score than the upper middle class in these more formal styles. In less formal styles, however (where Labov argues less attention is paid to speech and pronunciation is therefore less under the speaker's control), the lower middle class, like the two working-class groups, uses proportionately few of the prestige variant. This results in the line which joins lower middle class scores **crossing over** the line joining upper middle-class scores.

The behaviour of the lower middle class here, reflected in their scores, is known as **hypercorrection**. The most famous example of hypercorrection is that of post-vocalic (r) in New York City, as analysed by Labov (1972a). The variable post-vocalic (r) involves pronunciation or non-pronunciation of (r) in words such as *car* or *guard*, where (r) occurs after a vowel. Figure 4.4 below reproduces Labov's diagram. Only two variants are involved: presence or absence of post-vocalic (r) (for example, /kɑr/ or /kɑː/). A score of 100 represents consistent usage of (r) after a vowel; a score of 0 represents consistent absence of (r). Labov's informants were divided into six groups, and their speech measured in five different styles.

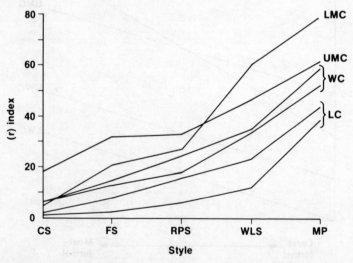

Figure 4.4: Social stratification of a linguistic variable in process of change: post-vocalic (r) in New York City (Labov 1972a:114)

This diagram reveals clearly that, while in less formal styles only the UMC uses the prestigious post-vocalic (r) with any degree of consistency, in the more formal styles LMC usage surpasses that of the UMC. The reason for hypercorrection seems to be the sensitivity of the LMC as a group to social pressures: their insecurity (because of their position on the borderline between the middle and working classes) is reflected in their concern with correctness and speaking 'properly'. When a linguistic variable is in the process of change, Labov argues, the LMC becomes sensitive to the use of the new prestige variant (in this case, use of post-vocalic (r)). In more formal styles (i.e. when paying more attention to speech) they make a conscious effort to speak 'correctly', and style-shift sharply from a virtually r-less casual (informal) style to a keeping-up-with-the-Jones', more r-full formal style.

4.3   SEX DIFFERENCES

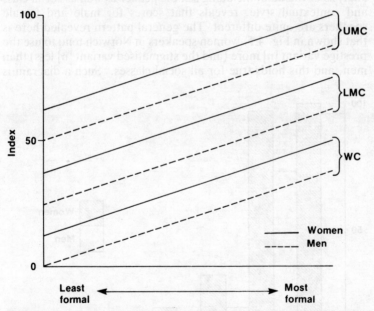

Figure 4.5: A diagrammatic representation of stratification according to social class and sex

Most early sociolinguistic work was concerned primarily with social class differences. However, it was soon apparent that other non-linguistic variables, such as ethnic group, age, and sex, were involved in structured linguistic variation. In the case of sex, it was established that in many speech communities female speakers will use a higher proportion of prestige forms than male speakers. In other words, the prestige norms seem to exert a stronger influence on women than on men. In the case of stable linguistic variables, we can expect a pattern like the one shown in Fig. 4.5 above. In the case of linguistic variables in the process of change, it appears that LMC *women* are particularly sensitive to the new prestige variant and are therefore prone to hypercorrection. Let us look at four examples of sociolinguistic research where sex differences have emerged as significant, to examine in detail the form such differences take. (The relationship between sex differences in speech and linguistic change will be taken up in Chapter 8.)

4.3.1 Norwich

Trudgill's demonstration of social stratification in the case of the variable (ng) in Norwich has been given in Fig. 4.2. A closer analysis of the data, including sex of speaker as well as social class and contextual style, reveals that scores for male and female speakers are quite different. The general pattern revealed here is that shown in Fig. 4.5: women speakers in Norwich tend to use the prestige variant [ŋ] more (and the stigmatised variant [n] less) than men, and this holds true for all social classes.[2] Such a diagram is

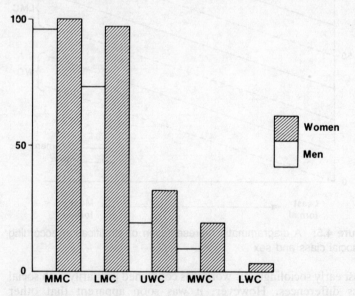

Figure 4.6: Histogram for (ng) in Norwich, showing social class and sex differences (based on Trudgill 1974a:94)

highly complex and difficult to read; Fig. 4.6 gives the results for formal style only, in histogram form. The contrast between the scores of women and men of the same social class is very striking.

Table 4.1 gives the actual scores of women and men in five social class groups and in four styles. As in Fig. 4.2, a score of 100 represents consistent [ŋ] pronunciation (the prestige form), and a score of 0 represents consistent use of [n] (the stigmatised variant). The most interesting point to notice is that in 14 out of 20 cases (i.e. 70 per cent) women's scores are higher than men's scores.

Table 4.1: The variable (ng) in Norwich – index scores broken down by social class, sex and contextual style* (based on Trudgill 1974a:94)

		CS	FS	RPS	WLS
MMC	M	69	96	100	100
	F	100	100	100	100
LMC	M	83	73	80	100
	F	33	97	100	100
UWC	M	5	19	82	100
	F	23	32	87	89
MWC	M	3	9	57	76
	F	12	19	54	80
LWC	M	0	0	0	34
	F	0	3	46	83

* I have reversed Trudgill's scores for consistency's sake (i.e. to keep 100 as the score representing the most prestigious pronunciation).

Among other things these figures tell us the following:

1. in all styles, women tend to use fewer stigmatised forms than men;

2. in formal contexts (where Trudgill got informants to read lists of words) women seem to be more sensitive to the prestige pattern than men (look at the last column – the lowest score for women is 80);

3. lower middle-class *women* style-shift very sharply: in the least formal style, they use quite a high proportion of the stigmatised variant, but in the three more formal styles, they correct their speech to correspond to that of the class above them (the middle middle-class) – Labov argues (1972a:243) that extreme style-shifting of this kind, often resulting in hypercorrection, is particularly marked in LMC women;

4. use of non-standard forms (that is, of the vernacular) seems to be associated not only with working-class speakers, but also with *male* speakers.

4.3.2 Glasgow

Ronald Macaulay's (1977;1978) study of Glasgow English revealed a similar pattern (though Macaulay's results are based on one style only, that of the formal interview). The diagram for the variable (i), as in *hit, kill, risk*, is given below in histogram form. A score of 100 represents consistent pronunciation of (i) as [ɪ] (the prestige form); a score of 0 represents consistent pronunciation of (i) as [ʌˆ] (Glasgow vernacular form).

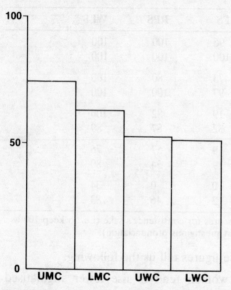

Figure 4.7: Social stratification of (i) in Glasgow (based on Macaulay 1978:135)

The diagram showing social class stratification presents the usual tidy picture: each social class group uses proportionately more of the prestige form than the next group down in the social class hierarchy. When the figures are broken down into male and female scores, however, as in Fig. 4.8, this superficial tidiness disappears. Women in each social class are revealed as using more of the prestige form [ɪ] than men of the same social class. Note that the women in each social class pattern like the men in the group *above* them. Conversely, the men in each social class pattern like the women in the group *below* them. (see Table 4.2, opposite).

66

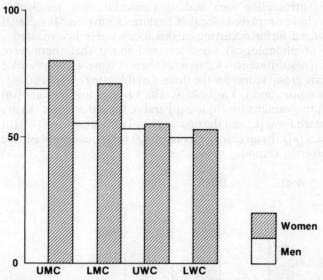

Figure 4.8: Stratification of (i) by social class and sex (based on Macaulay 1978:135)

Table 4.2: Male and female scores for (i) in Glasgow (based on Macaulay 1978:135)

	Men	Women
UMC	69.00	80.00
LMC	55.25	71.25
UWC	53.25	55.00
LWC	50.00	53.00

Macaulay pointed out that the major break in the women's scores comes between the lower middle class and the upper working class, while for men it comes between the upper middle class and the lower middle class. So LMC women speak more like UMC women, while LMC men speak more like UWC men. This shows yet again the pivotal nature of the lower middle class.

Macaulay's data, like Trudgill's, suggests that social class scores conceal more than they reveal. In the case of the variable (i) in Glasgow, social class scores give us only an average of male and female scores, and fail to differentiate male and female usage.

4.3.3 West Wirral

Mark Newbrook's (1982) study of West Wirral aims to establish how far the urban vernacular of Liverpool ('Scouse') has spread

67

into the surrounding area and, in particular, how far Scouse features have replaced local Cheshire forms as the usual non-standard forms occurring in this locality. He investigated a number of phonological variables, and found that there were significant sex differences for most of them. Figure 4.9 shows male and female group scores for the three variables (ing) as in *jumping*, (h) as in *house*, and (k) as in *kick*. The variants for (ing) are [ɪŋ] and [ɪn]; the variants for (h) are [h] and ø; the variants for (k) are the standard form [k] and the non-standard affricated form [kˣ] (or sometimes [x]). In all cases, a score of 100 indicates consistent use of the prestige variant.

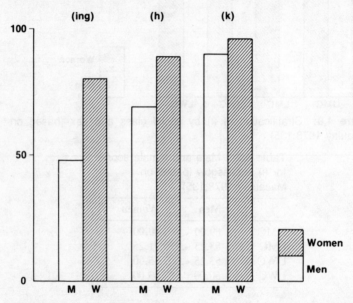

Figure 4.9: Sex differences in West Wirral for three phonological variables: (ing), (h) and (k)

With all three variables, we find the expected pattern: women's pronunciation is closer to the prestige standard than men's. Moreover, these group scores conceal the fact that the range of individual scores involved differs greatly between men and women. The typical score for a working-class man was much lower than that for a middle-class man, whereas women's scores covered a much narrower range. This suggests that social class is a more important factor in determining men's speech than women's, at least in West Wirral.

Below (Fig. 4.10) is the histogram for the variable (a) as in *bath*, *grass*. In this case, informants are analysed in terms of age as well as sex. A score of 100 represents consistent RP pronunciation: [ɑ:]; a score of 0 represents consistent non-standard pronunciation :[æ]. Note that women's scores are higher than men's in each age

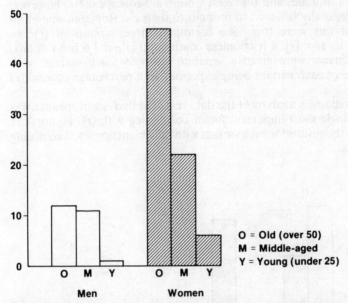

Figure 4.10: The variable (a) in West Wirral showing stratification by age and sex

group. Note also the age-grading that occurs with this variable: scores are higher for older speakers than for younger ones. Older *women* are much closer to the standard norms than other speakers, while young men are virtually consistent [æ] users. It looks as if young women are participating in the increasing dominance of [æ]. This non-standard variant seems to be a marker not only of male speech, but also of the speech of the young.

4.3.4 Edinburgh

Our fourth example is taken from Suzanne Romaine's (1978) work in Edinburgh. Her study was confined to primary-school children with working class fathers; each child was interviewed alone, and the 10-year olds also read a passage. Note that this study is more selective than the others we have looked at: informants belong to a narrow age range (6–10 years), to the working class (as far as father's occupation can be said to define this) and the data is obtained in one context only (with the exception of the 10-year olds).

One of the variables included in Romaine's investigation was postvocalic (r) as in *car, door*, etc. South of the Scottish border, this variable is found only in rural mid-north Lancashire and in the Welsh Marches and the West Country; Scots speakers, however, are generally believed to pronounce their r's. Romaine wanted to see if this were true. She identified three variants of (r): an alveolar tap: [ɾ], a frictionless continuant: [ɹ], and ø (no r at all). Informants were given a separate score for each variant, with usage of each variant being expressed as a percentage of total (r) use.

Romaine's analysis of the data revealed that sex of speaker was the single most important factor correlating with (r). Figure 4.11 gives the results for each variant with informants grouped according to sex.

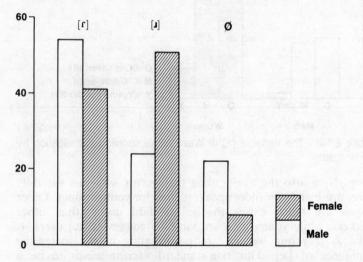

Figure 4.11: Sex differences in the use of the variable (r) in Edinburgh (based on Romaine 1978:150)

This histogram conflates the scores of children in the three age groups investigated, since clear-cut differences in the use of (r) emerged between male and female speakers in each age group. Note that male speakers consistently use more of the [ɾ] variant than female speakers, and are also more likely to use ø. Girls on the other hand consistently prefer the frictionless continuant [ɹ]; girls, moreover, seem to avoid r-less pronunciation.

This variable, then, again reveals sharp sex differentiation. In terms of frequency, the most striking feature is the girls' use of [ɹ]. Clearly [ɹ] is a marker of female speech in Edinburgh.

70

4.3.5 Summary

These four British studies show us the regularity of sex differentiation in speech. Where variation exists, it often seems to be the case that male and female speakers prefer different variants. Further, where it is possible to label one of the variants as prestigious, then it is typically *female* speakers who are found to use this variant. This was the case with Norwich (ng), Glasgow (i) and West Wirral (ing), (h) and (k). Use of non-standard, non-prestige forms, in other words, seems to be associated not only with working-class speakers, but also with *male* speakers. Where we find a given variant consistently used by one set of speakers rather than by another, we call that variant a **marker**. Our examples show us that [n] is a marker of male speech in Norwich, that [æ] is a marker of male speech (and of younger speakers) in the Wirral, and that [ɹ] is a marker of female speech in Edinburgh.

4.4 EXPLANATIONS

The examples given above, all taken from sociolinguistic work in Britain, show us the form that linguistic variation between the sexes takes. This brings us to the question, Why? The main goal of quantitative studies such as those used as examples in this chapter is the collection and analysis of data on linguistic variation. Many sociolinguists are not primarily concerned with *why* such variation exists, and their methodology is not usually designed to probe such questions.

4.4.1 Women's sensitivity to linguistic norms

Women's sensitivity to linguistic norms is often asserted, and this is attributed to their insecure social position. Such insecurity on the part of women offers a clear parallel with the lower middle class, who, as we saw in 4.2.2, provide the classic example of hypercorrect linguistic behaviour. Are sociolinguists really saying that women's linguistic behaviour is hypercorrect?[3] Let us look at some examples.

1. *(ng) in Norwich*
   Besides showing a regular pattern of sex differentiation, Table 4.1 (index scores for (ng) in Norwich) also exemplifies the extreme style-shifting of LMC women. In formal styles, LMC women pattern like the UMC as a whole, but in more informal speech they use a high proportion of stigmatised forms.

2. *the glottal stop in Glasgow*
   The glottal stop is the most overtly stigmatised feature

71

of Glasgow speech. Macaulay found that it was widely used, but with clear social stratification (working-class groups using it considerably more than middle-class groups). The biggest contrast was between LMC men and women: LMC female informants used 40 per cent fewer glottal stops than LMC male informants. One LMC woman used fewer glottal stops than *any* UMC informant – clearly hypercorrect usage.

3. *(o) on Merseyside*
   This linguistic variable – which occurs in words like *coat, go* – has many variants. One of these, [ɛʊ], is generally considered to be hypercorrect.[4] In his work in West Wirral, Newbrook established that, when they used Scouse variants, a minority of male informants but *all* the females preferred this variant.

The first two examples show that the hypercorrect pattern of the second highest status group, the lower middle class, is crucially connected with the usage of LMC *women*. The third example shows a more general pattern; since Newbrook did not classify informants by social class we cannot be sure whether LMC women were particularly sensitive to [ɛʊ]. But these examples, and the material examined earlier in this chapter, do not justify labelling women's speech as a whole as hypercorrect. As Fig. 4.5 shows, sex differences lead to regular stratification, with women using fewer stigmatised forms and more prestige forms than men in each social class. It is no more justifiable to call this pattern of female usage hypercorrect than it would be to call the usage of the middle class hypercorrect in relation to that of the working class.

4.4.2 Self-evaluation tests

In order to test sensitivity to linguistic norms, Trudgill (1972;1974a) carried out self-evaluation tests on his informants. He presented them with a recording of certain words, with two or more different pronunciations, varying from prestigious pronunciation (RP) to non-standard Norwich pronunciation. Informants were asked to indicate which of the forms most closely resembled the one they habitually used. The variables (er), as in *ear, here, idea*, and (a) as in *gate, face, name*, were both involved in this test. In the case of (er), only 28 per cent of male informants and 18 per cent of female informants responded accurately (that is, claimed to use the form which corresponded to their actual usage in Casual Speech, as recorded in the interview). A staggering 68 per cent of the women (and 22 per cent of the men) **over-reported**, that is, claimed to use the prestige form when their index scores revealed they actually didn't. On the other hand, half the men (50 per cent) and 14 per cent of the women **under-reported**, that is, they claimed to use non-standard forms when their index scores revealed that they habitually used forms closer to standard pronunciation.

The results for the variable (a) repeat this pattern. 50 per cent of the men and 57 per cent of the women evaluate their pronunciation accurately. 43 per cent of the women (and 22 per cent of the men) *over*-report, while 28 per cent of the men (and none of the women) *under*-report. Table 4.3 summarises these figures.

Table 4.3 Percentage scores for self-evaluation for (er) and (a) in Norwich (based on Trudgill 1972)

	(er)		(a)	
	M	**F**	**M**	**F**
Over-report	22	68	22	43
Under-report	50	14	28	0
Accurate	28	18	50	57

The first thing to notice is that Trudgill's test reveals significant *over*-reporting by *women*. This suggests that women *are* sensitive to prestige norms. Many women in Norwich believe that they are producing forms close to standard pronunciation when they are not. This suggests that they are *aiming at* standard pronunciation, and that they are trying to avoid stigmatised forms.

The second thing to notice is that Trudgill's test reveals significant *under*-reporting by *men*. They claim to use non-standard forms when in fact they do not. Such behaviour can be explained by hypothesising that non-standard speech must have **covert prestige**.

4.4.3 Covert prestige

The concept of covert prestige arose when linguists attempted to explain the persistence of vernacular (non-standard) forms in the speech of working-class speakers. In view of the resistance of working-class speakers to Standard English (assuming they want to speak as they do), we have to postulate the existence of another set of norms – vernacular norms – which have covert prestige and therefore exert a powerful influence on linguistic behaviour. In the light of Trudgill's self-evaluation tests and the examples of male/female differences given earlier in the chapter, it seems reasonable to assume that vernacular forms have covert prestige not just for the working class but also for *men*. Under-reporting is equally common among middle-class men as among working-class men in Norwich. It looks as if many Norwich men are actually aiming at non-standard working-class speech.

We see here the development of a stronger explanatory model. Early work on sex differences in language emphasised women's apparent sensitivity to prestige forms. The concept of prestige as a force which attracts different speakers more or less powerfully depending on their sex is supported by the sociolinguistic evidence: men do indeed use fewer prestige forms than women. But the introduction of the concept of covert prestige strengthens the model, by postulating the existence of two opposing sets of norms competing for speakers' loyalty: Standard English with its overt prestige, and vernacular norms with covert prestige. It is claimed that women are attracted by the norms of Standard English while men respond to the covert prestige of the vernacular. This model is also used to explain social class differences – in other words, it is argued that social class differences in language exist because middle-class speakers give allegiance to the institutionalised norms of Standard English while working-class speakers reject these norms and instead give allegiance to the vernacular. This reveals an interesting parallelism between women and the middle class, on the one hand, and men and the working class, on the other.

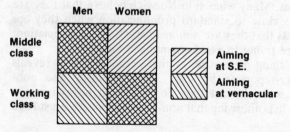

Figure 4.12: The intersection of social class, sex and language

Middle-class *women* and working-class *men* have no conflict of interests. Both their sex and their social class point to the same affiliation. For middle-class men and working-class women, however, there is a conflict of interests: the behaviour predictable on the basis of their social class will be incompatible with the behaviour predictable on the basis of their sex.

The ambiguity of the position of middle-class male speakers and working-class female speakers is nicely pinpointed by the results of the following experiment (Edwards 1979a). Adult judges were presented with tape recordings of twenty middle-class and twenty working-class children and asked to identify the sex of the child from their speech. In a minority of cases, the judges were not able to do this accurately. As Fig. 4.13 shows, the judges did not make random mistakes; they made mistakes about two sets of children: middle-class boys and working-class girls. Middle-class boys sounded like girls to the judges, while working-class girls sounded like boys.

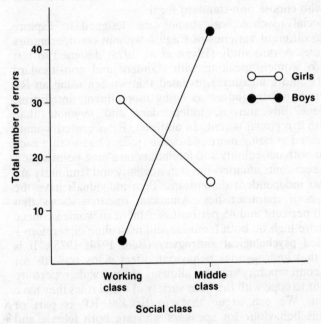

Figure 4.13: Interaction between sex and social class of children in terms of errors of sex identification (Edwards 1979:93)

4.4.4 Status and solidarity

These explanations themselves require explanations. If we accept that, in speech communities such as those described in this chapter, speakers choose between opposing sets of linguistic norms, we still have to explain why it is that women are more likely to be influenced by the publicly legitimised standard norms, and that men are more likely to be influenced by vernacular norms which are not publicly recognised.

Social psychologists have studied attitudes to speech in some detail. Their research confirms that RP has far more prestige than regional accents in Britain. One of the 'rewards' (to use the social psychologists' term) for speakers who use speech closer to standard norms is that they acquire greater **status**. Another reward seems to be that RP speakers are perceived as being more ambitious, more intelligent and more self-confident. However, while RP speakers are rated highly in terms of competence, regionally accented speakers are rated highly in terms of personal attractiveness: they are perceived to be serious, talkative, good-natured, and as having a sense of humour. This suggests that there are also rewards, though of a different kind, for those speakers who choose non-standard forms.

Most social psychological studies are designed to explore attitudes to different varieties of English without considering sex as a variable. A rare study (Elyan et al. 1978) designed to test reactions to women speaking with standard and non-standard accents (RP and Lancashire) revealed that women using an RP accent were rated by judges as being more fluent, intelligent, self-confident, adventurous, independent and *feminine* than women with a regional accent. In addition, RP-accented women were also rated as being more *masculine* (judges had to rate each speaker for both masculinity and femininity on a nine-point scale). This may seem contradictory, but if masculinity and femininity are seen as two independent dimensions, then individuals have the choice of both characteristics. American research shows that between 30 per cent and 45 per cent of American women college students score high on both feminine and masculine dimensions – this is called **psychological androgyny** (Bem 1974; 1975). It is suggested that androgynous behaviour offers many rewards for women in contemporary society, allowing them a wide repertoire of behaviour to cope with the wide variety of social roles they have to take on. We can argue that, in Britain, RP is part of androgynous behaviour for speakers who are both female and middle-class, because of these rewards.

Speakers, however, are not isolated individuals; they are members of social groups, and it is one of language's functions to act as a symbol of group identity. For all sorts of reasons, working-class speakers diverge linguistically from middle-class speakers, in order to mark the social distance between the two groups. At the same time, working-class speakers will converge linguistically with each other, in order to show **solidarity**, to mark their membership of the same social group. The conscious effort by members of the working class *not* to speak Standard English is well documented, as the following quotations demonstrate:

1. '. . . you'd get battered off a' the pals . . .'
   (George W., Edinburgh, in response to a suggestion that he should 'talk nice', quoted in Reid 1978).

2. A Cockney grandmother claimed her grandson would

76

be labelled 'a queer' if he talked with a 'la-di-da' accent (quoted in Bragg & Ellis 1976).

3. 'I don't think I would change the way I speak. I wouldn't like to have an English accent. I think it's a very daft one. They pronounce words correctly but they don't sound very nice. In your own environment you'd feel out of place. If you live in Glasgow you must talk like a Glaswegian'
(15-year-old Glasgow boy, quoted by Macaulay 1977).

Notice that all these examples come from *male* speakers. There are clearly very strong pressures on speakers who are both working-class and male to diverge from Standard English. By using non-standard forms, male speakers signal their solidarity with each other.

Social groups need to assert their distinctiveness, and language is one way of doing this. It looks as though there are strong cultural pressures on men and women to distinguish themselves from each other, even though other groupings (such as social class, ethnic group, age) notionally place them together. It is important for groups to maintain their identity, and language variation contributes to this in two ways:

1. Linguistic differences strengthen in-group unity (that is, members of a group recognise each other as being linguistically *similar* to each other and *different* from people outside the group);

2. Linguistic differences increase the distance between groups (which helps to maintain distinctive group identities).

So linguistic differences between women and men can be seen as functioning to maintain their separate identities.

4.4.5 Conclusion

In this chapter we have looked at some examples of sociolinguistic research which demonstrate sex differentiation, and we have discussed some of the reasons put forward to explain this phenomenon. In all known communities, male and female are important categories; that is, members of a community are distinguished from each other in terms of *sex*, as well as in other (more culture-specific) ways. Not surprisingly, in sociolinguistic research, sex has emerged as an important variable, and sociologuists have found that sex differences in language often cut across social class variation. Women – like middle-class speakers – are shown to use proportionately more standard forms (those accorded overt prestige by society), while men – like working-class speakers – are shown to use proportionately more non-standard forms. Why women should regularly select forms closer to Standard English, while men select forms closer to the vernacular, is a phenomenon which is still little understood. The next chapter will look at work which explores the hypothesis that the level of integration of speakers in a community will be directly reflected in their language, and will show in what ways such work refines our understanding of male/female differences in language.

NOTES

1 Note that to pass O level English Language, arguably the most crucial subject at O level, pupils must have internalised these concepts, and must have acquired a facility in written Standard English.

2 This rests on the assumption that the men's and women's social class has been accurately assessed. However, since Trudgill, like most other researchers, assessed women's social class partly on the occupation of their husband or father, it is not clear that this assumption is justified.

3 See, for example, Labov 1972a:243.

4 Note that this is a different kind of hypercorrection since the variant is never used by UMC informants: it is a qualitative rather than a quantitative overshoot. Knowles (1974) and De Lyon (1981) both consider [ɛʊ] to be hypercorrect on Merseyside, but Newbrook (who refers to it as [ɤ̟ʊ]) feels it is not synchronically hypercorrect in West Wirral.

Chapter Five

Social networks

5.1 THE CONCEPT OF SOCIAL NETWORK

One of the most fruitful explanations of linguistic variation in recent years has been the concept of social network. This concept has been current in the social sciences for some years, but was not mentioned in sociolinguistic analysis until Blom and Gumperz (1972), and not well known before publication of the Milroys' Belfast study (Milroy & Milroy 1978; Milroy 1980).

Members of a given speech community – such as Belfast – can be seen as being connected to each other in social networks which may be relatively 'closed' or 'open'. An individual whose personal contacts all know each other belongs to a closed network (see Fig. 5.1). The arrows represent mutual knowing.

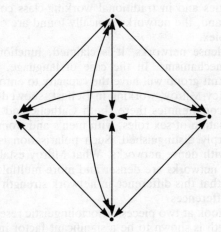

Figure 5.1: A closed network

An individual whose personal contacts tend not to know each other belongs to an open network (see Fig. 5.2).

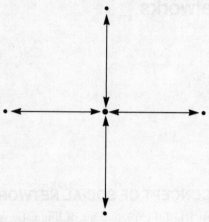

Figure 5.2: An open network

Closed networks are said to be of **high density**; open networks are said to be of **low density**. Moreover, the links between people may be of different kinds: people can relate to each other as relatives, as neighbours, as workmates, as friends. Where individuals are linked in several ways, e.g. by job, family and leisure activities, then the network ties are said to be **multiplex**.

It seems that the networks typically found in socially mobile, highly industrialised societies are of low density and **uniplex** (that is, individuals are not linked in more than one way). In rural village communities and in traditional working-class communities, on the other hand, the networks typically found are of high density and multiplex.

Relatively dense networks, it is claimed, function as norm-enforcement mechanisms. In the case of language, this means that a closely-knit group will have the capacity to enforce *linguistic* norms. Lesley Milroy, working in Belfast, showed that in the working-class communities there (both Catholic and Protestant) there is polarisation of sex roles, with men's and women's activities being sharply distinguished. Such polarisation is typical of communities with dense networks. What Milroy established was that the men's networks are denser and more multiplex than the women's, and that this difference in network strength is matched by linguistic differences.

Let us now look at two pieces of sociolinguistic research where network strength is shown to be a significant factor in predicting male/female differences, starting with Lesley Milroy's work on

Belfast, and then considering Jenny Cheshire's study of adolescents in Reading.[1]

5.1.1 Belfast

Milroy investigated three working-class communities in Belfast: Balymacarrett (a Protestant area in East Belfast), the Hammer (a Protestant area in West Belfast) and the Clonard (a Catholic area in West Belfast). All three areas are poor working-class districts with a high incidence of unemployment.

Milroy's analysis of these communities was based not on interviews but on **participant observation**. Through informal contacts with core members of these communities, she was able to approach them in the capacity of 'a friend of a friend'. This role meant that she was accepted with friendliness and trust; it also enabled her to observe and participate in prolonged and informal interaction. Her tape recorder was soon accepted in the various households she visited, and she could be reasonably confident that the conversations she recorded were representative of the vernacular.

She observed not only the language of the people she contacted, but also their social networks. Because all three communities revealed dense and multiplex networks, she decided to give each individual a Network Strength Score, depending on five factors. Scores for each individual were calculated by assigning one point for each condition fulfilled. The five factors were as follows:

1. Belonging to a high-density, territorially-based group.

2. Having substantial ties of kinship in the neighbourhood (more than one household in addition to the nuclear family).

3. Working at the same place as at least two others from the same area.

4. Working at the same place as at least two others of the same sex from the area.

5. Associating voluntarily with workmates in leisure hours.

The total score was designed to reflect the individual's level of integration into localised networks.

Individual scores, then, ranged from 0 to 5. As will be apparent, factors 3, 4, and 5 will give high scores to men in traditional employment. In Ballymacarrett, where traditional employment patterns still prevail to some extent (the men working in the shipyards), the men typically had high scores. In the Hammer and

81

Clonard, on the other hand, which are both areas of high *male* unemployment, individual women often scored as high as or higher than men.

The value of the social network as a concept, and of the Network Strength Score as an analytical tool, lies in their ability to demonstrate a correlation between the integration of an individual in the community, and the way that individual speaks. Individuals who participate in close-knit networks are also those who most consistently use vernacular forms in speech. It would be a common-sense assumption that the speech of members of a close-knit group would tend to be more homogeneous than that of members of a loosely knit group; the Network Strength Scale allied with linguistic analysis allows the assumption to be examined more closely.

The variable (th)

One of the variables examined by Milroy was the interdental voiced fricative (t) occurring intervocalically in words such as *mother, bother, together*. Vernacular speakers in Belfast delete (th) in such words; they pronounce *mother*, for example, as [mɔ.ər]. In the following diagram, (Fig. 5.3), a score of 0 represents consistent pronunciation of (th) intervocalically, while

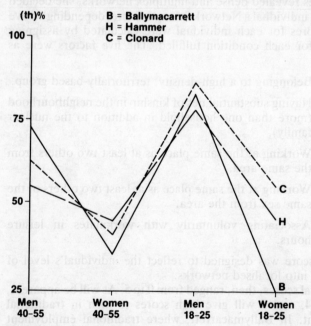

Figure 5.3: The distribution of (th) by age, sex, and area in Belfast (Milroy 1980:128)

82

100 represents consistent deletion of (th); note that a score of 100 now represents consistent *vernacular* pronunciation. Both studies described in this chapter focus on working-class communities and their speech. Their scoring is therefore the inverse of that used in the previous chapter: speakers are measured against the set of norms which constitute the vernacular, not against the set of norms known as Standard English. The diagram shows the distribution of (th) by age, sex and area.

This variable shows the pattern typical of stable sociolinguistic markers. All three communities are revealed as sharing the same attitude to (th). The sex differences are very marked, pariculariy in Ballymacarrett, the most traditional of the three areas. The two generations are shown to pattern similarly, though men's and women's pronunciation is more polarised in the younger generation, with higher scores for 18–25 year-old men and low scores for 18–25 year-old women (particularly Ballymacarrett women).

It's important to consider individual scores as well as group scores. In the three communities, individual scores confirm the striking sex differentiation of intervocalic (th) – the men's and women's scores do not overlap at all. Even the men with the lowest scores (the men who delete (th) least) score more than the women with the highest scores. In other words, even the men whose pronunciation is furthest from the vernacular norms delete (th) intervocalically more than any woman.

The variable (a)

This pattern is not found with all variables, however. Consider Fig. 5.4, for the variable (a).

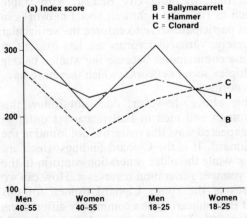

Figure 5.4: The distribution of (a) by age, sex and area in Belfast (Milroy 1980:124)

83

This is a much more complex variable, since it cannot be scored in the simple binary fashion that (th) was. A five-point scale was used to measure the degree of retraction and back-raising of (a) in words like *hat*, *man*, *back*, with a score of 1 for [æ] ranging through [a], [ä], [ɑ] to a score of 5 for [ɔə]. (The higher the score, the greater the backing of (a).) First, consider the pattern for Ballymacarrett. As we saw with (th), there is clear sex differentiation in this community, with the same zig-zag line as before. The Hammer and the Clonard, however, do not show this pattern. In the Hammer, the difference between the sexes for (a) is insignificant, while in the Clonard, the *young women* use *more* backed variants of (a) than the young men (quite unlike the older women, whose scores are significantly lower than those of the men of their generation, following the usual pattern).

So what do the data on these two variables in Belfast tell us? First, for certain stable variables such as (th), there is clear differentiation between the sexes. As earlier sociolinguistic studies had established, this difference is the result of the men using variants consistently closer to the vernacular norms, and of the women using variants consistently less close. Milroy suggests as an explanation of this difference that men in working-class inner city areas belong to denser, more multiplex networks than women. By using her Network Strength Scale, she was able to show that a high Network Strength Score was clearly correlated with use of the vernacular. In most cases, this meant that men whose speech revealed high usage of vernacular forms were also found to belong to tight-knit social networks. If it is accepted that social networks operate as important norm-enforcing mechanisms, then it would seem to be the case that, in inner city Belfast, with stable linguistic variables such as (th), the tight-knit social networks in which most of the men participate serve to enforce the vernacular speech norms. Conversely, vernacular forms are less evident in women's speech in these communities because the women belong to less dense, less multiplex social networks, which therefore have less power to enforce norms.

The second variable above, however, does not follow this pattern. While the women and men in Ballymacarrett differ in their use of (a) in the expected way, this pattern is not found in the Hammer or in the Clonard. It is the Clonard findings which are particularly interesting: while the older generation conform to the expected pattern, the younger generation reverses it. How can we explain the high scores of the young Clonard women for this variable? It seems that Ballymacarrett as a community differs from the other two: it suffers little from male unemployment, largely because of its location by the shipyards. The Hammer and the

Clonard both had unemployment rates of around 35 per cent at the time of Milroy's research, which clearly affected social relationships. Men from these areas were forced to look for work outside the community, and also shared more in domestic tasks (with consequent blurring of sex roles). The women in these areas went out to work and, in the case of the young Clonard women, all worked together. This meant that the young Clonard women, by contrast with all the other female groups, belonged to a dense and multiplex network; they lived, worked and amused themselves together. The young Clonard women have the highest network score of any sub-group (mean = 4.75); the mean for the young Clonard men is 3.0. This is in complete contrast with the scores for Ballymacarrett, where the mean network score for men is 3.96, compared with 1.33 for the women. The contrast is between a traditional working-class community (Ballymacarrett) and a working-class community undergoing social change because of severe male unemployment (Clonard). The tight-knit network to which the young Clonard women belong clearly exerts pressure on its members, who are linguistically homogeneous. Because of their social circumstances, the young Clonard women are linguistically more like the young Ballymacarrett men than like the other women in the three communities. Social networks in this case help to explain not only linguistic differences between the sexes, but also the seemingly divergent behaviour of the younger Clonard women.

5.1.2 Reading

It seems to be the case that social networks are most close-knit around the age of sixteen. This means that adolescents will be more consistent vernacular speakers than adults. Labov's famous study of Black English Vernacular focused on adolescent peer groups in New York (Labov 1972b), and Cheshire's more recent work in Reading was based on three groups of adolescents. While Labov studied only male peer groups, Cheshire studied both boys and girls, which enabled her to examine sex differentiation in vernacular usage.

Cheshire, like Labov and Milroy, gained her data through long-term participant observation. That is, having decided to analyse the speech of working-class adolescent peer groups, she located three groups (two of boys, one of girls) in two adventure playgrounds in Reading, and was gradually accepted by them. (She told the first group that she had a vacation job, finding out what people in Reading thought of the town. They sympathised with her need to earn some money and accepted the tape recorder as an aid to her supposedly poor memory.) She visited the playgrounds two or three times a week for nine months, and was soon on very friendly terms with the adolescents. She took care, through details like informal dress and riding a motor-bike, to reduce the social distance between the adolescents and herself as far as possible.

Cheshire examined non-standard morphological and syntactic features in the speech of the adolescents. Examples of eleven of these variables are given below.

1. non-standard -s
   'They calls me all the names under the sun, don't they?' (Derek)

2. non-standard has
   'You just has to do what the teachers tell you.' (Mandy)

3. non-standard was
   'You was with me, wasn't you? (Ann)

4. negative concord
   'It ain't got no pedigree or nothing.' (Nobby)

5. non-standard never
   'I never went to school today' (Lynne)

6. non-standard what
   'Are you the little bastards what hit my son over the head?' (Nobby)

7. non-standard do
   'She cadges, she do.' (Julie)

8. non-standard come
   'I come down here yesterday.'

9. ain't = auxiliary have
   'I ain't seen my Nan for nearly seven years.' (Tracey)

10. ain't = auxiliary be
    'Course I ain't going to the Avenue.' (Mandy)

11. ain't = copula
    'You ain't no boss.' (Rob)

The table below gives percentage scores for male and female speakers for these eleven variables. A score of 100 represents consistent use of the non-standard forms. The non-standard forms are all used less often by the girls than by the boys, apart from non-standard do, a feature which seems to be involved in linguistic change. These findings, then, conform to the expected pattern, with female speakers adhering more closely to standard norms, while male speakers use non-standard forms more consistently.

In terms of the social networks they belong to, it seems that the boys belong to structured peer groups of the kind described by

Table 5.1: Sex differences in non-standard features of Reading speech (Cheshire 1982b:163)

	Frequency indices	
	Boys	**Girls**
nonstandard **-s**	53.16	52.04
nonstandard **has**	54.76	51.61
nonstandard **was**	88.15	73.58
negative concord	88.33	51.85
nonstandard **never**	46.84	40.00
nonstandard **what**	36.36	14.58
nonstandard **do**	57.69	78.95
nonstandard **come**	100.00	75.33
ain't = aux **have**	92.00	64.58
ain't = aux **be**	74.19	42.11
ain't = copula	85.83	61.18

Labov in his work with black adolescents in New York, while the girls belong to a much less tightly knit group. The sociometric diagram (Fig. 5.5) shows the friendship patterns obtaining between the boys in the Orts Road group. Each boy was asked

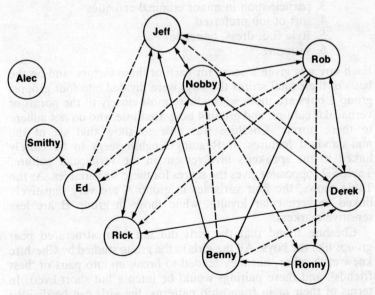

Figure 5.5: Friendship patterns in the Orts Road group (Cheshire 1982a:89)

which friends he spent most of his time with; solid lines represent reciprocal naming and thus the main social links within the group.

On the basis of the boys' responses, Cheshire divided them into three groups: core members, secondary members, and non-members. Cheshire investigated the relationship between use of non-standard linguistic features and peer group status. She found some positive correlations: of the nine most frequently occurring non-standard features in the boys' speech, six were used more by core members than by others, and four of the features (non-standard present tense forms, *has*, *was*, and *never*) were used most by core members and least by non-members. But this correlation is not as regular and systematic as that found by Labov in his work on black adolescent peer groups. It seems that adolescent peer groups in Britain have a more flexible structure. The hierarchically structured and tight-knit adolescent groups in New York show a corresponding high correlation between peer group status and use of non-standard language. Cheshire also suggests that not *all* the non-standard features of Reading English necessarily serve as markers of peer group status. In order to investigate *which* variables function as markers of vernacular loyalty, she constructed a vernacular culture index, based on the following six factors:

1. carrying of weapons
2. skill at fighting
3. participation in minor criminal activities
4. sort of job preferred
5. style (i.e. dress, hairstyle)
6. swearing.

Each boy was given a score for each of these factors, and on the basis of their total scores the boys were divided into four groups: group 1 boys are those who adhere most closely to the norms of vernacular culture, and group 4 boys are those who do not adhere to these norms. Cheshire was able to show that six of the non-standard features of Reading English seem to be closely linked to the speaker's involvement in the vernacular culture. Table 5.2 (opposite) gives the scores for these six variables. As the Table shows, the four variables in group A are very sensitively linked to vernacular loyalty, while those in group B are less sensitive markers.

Cheshire found that the girls did not form structured peer groups like the boys. All the girls in the group studied by Cheshire knew each other, but they tended to break up into pairs of 'best friends', and these pairings would be intense but short-lived. In terms of their main friendship patterns, the girls can be divided into three separate sub-groups, as shown in Fig. 5.6 (opposite).

Table 5.2 Adherence to vernacular culture – scores for frequency of occurrence of six non-standard forms (based on Cheshire 1982b:156)

		Group 1	Group 2	Group 3	Group 4
Class A	non-standard **-s**	77.36	54.03	36.57	21.21
	non-standard **has**	66.67	50.00	41.65	(33.33)*
	non-standard **was**	90.32	89.74	83.33	71.43
	negative concord	100.00	85.71	83.33	71.43
Class B	non-standard **never**	64.71	41.67	45.45	37.50
	non-standard **what**	92.31	7.69	33.33	0.00

* Number of occurrences of this variable was low, so the index score may be unreliable.

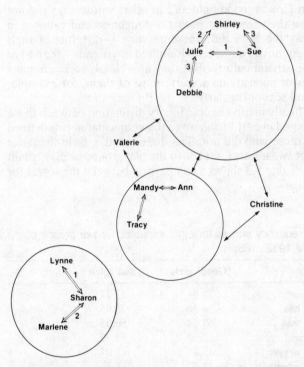

Figure 5.6: Friendship patterns in the Shinfield girls' group (Cheshire 1982a:93)

When asked who they spent most of their time with, each girl named her 'best friend' (double lines in Fig. 5.6). When asked who else they spent time with, they named all the other girls in the group, except for the three 'outsiders', Lynne, Marlene and Sharon, who form a separate sub-group. Valerie and Christine are also peripheral and spend less time at the playground: Valerie is older and gave her boyfriend's name in answer to the first question; Christine is younger and named a schoolfriend.

Cheshire found no systematic pattern of variation in language correlating with this rather unstructured pattern of relationships. Moreover, she decided that the vernacular culture index which she had used to measure the boys' adherence to vernacular values could not be used for the girls. Although the girls took part in activities which could be called delinquent, such as stealing and setting fire to the playground, their attitude to such activities differed from the boys'. They did not boast about what they had done, and although they had fights from time to time, they did not value certain girls as 'good fighters'. In other words, they did not seem to value the vernacular norms of toughness and violence in the same way the boys did. In some ways – in terms of their interest in pop music, films, television and boyfriends – they were closer to mainstream culture. But they also clearly rejected many of the values of mainstream society; most of them, for example, did not attend school regularly.

Cheshire finally made a simple binary distinction between those girls who seemed in part to adhere to the vernacular norms defined earlier, and those who did not. The three 'good' girls in the latter group did not swear, steal, set fire to the playground or play truant from school. Table 5.3 shows a comparison between the scores for the two groups.

Table 5.3 Frequency indices for eight variables for two groups of girls (Cheshire 1982b:163)

	'Good' girls	'Bad' girls
non-standard -s	25.84	57.27
non-standard **has**	36.36	35.85
non-standard **was**	63.64	80.95
negative concord	12.50	58.70
non-standard **never**	45.45	41.07
non-standard **what**	33.33	5.56
non-standard **come**	30.77	90.63
ain't = copula	14.29	67.12

As this table shows, there are five features which are used more by the 'bad' girls than by the 'good' ones: non-standard -s, was, come, negative concord, and ain't as copula. Three of these, as we saw earlier, function as markers of vernacular loyalty for boys too: non-standard -s suffix, was and negative concord. Non-standard come is, however, invariant for the boys (they all use it 100 per cent of the time) whereas it clearly functions as a marker of vernacular loyalty for the girls, being almost categorical for 'bad' girls, but occurring much less frequently in the speech of the three 'good' girls (30.77 per cent). Ain't too seems to function as a marker of vernacular loyalty for girls, but not for boys, who all use it with relatively similar frequency. Non-standard never and what function only loosely as markers of vernacular loyalty for the boys; for the girls they seem not to be markers at all, since the 'good' girls use them more.

Cheshire concludes that different speakers exploit the system in different ways. While some non-standard linguistic features act as markers of vernacular loyalty for both male and female adolescents in Reading (non-standard present tense verb forms, non-standard was, and negative concord), there are other non-standard features which act primarily as sex markers: that is, they function as markers of vernacular loyalty only for girls (non-standard come and ain't as a copula) or only for boys (non-standard never and what). These results implicitly challenge the notion that members of a speech community can be defined in terms of shared norms.

5.2   EXPLANATION IN THE LIGHT OF SOCIAL NETWORK THEORY

The concept of the social network, which enables us to see the individual in relation to the group, clearly refines our understanding of sex differences in language. The evidence is that a tight-knit network structure is an important mechanism of language maintenance. Men's speech in many speech communities is closer to the vernacular than women's, and we can see that it is the close-knit social networks to which men have traditionally belonged which serve to maintain vernacular speech norms. Women's speech, then, is closer to the standard not because women are deliberately aiming at Standard English but because the less tight-knit networks which women belong to are less efficient at enforcing vernacular norms. In other words, women may use forms closer to Standard English for the negative reason that they are relatively less exposed to vernacular speech and more exposed to Standard English.

Cheshire's examination of style-shifting in the speech of her informants gives us additional information on the nature of peer group pressure. She made a set of recordings in the schools attended by the adolescents in her groups, and she used this material to see whether the speech of the adolescents was affected by the more formal school context. She found that all three groups in her study used fewer non-standard verb forms in school (i.e. non-standard -*s*). Interestingly, it emerged that the girls' use of non-standard verb forms decreased more sharply than the boys'. We can infer from the fact that the girls were not part of a cohesive peer group, and that their friendships fluctuated frequently, that they are less under pressure from the group to use vernacular forms, and consequently more exposed to the prestige norms of Standard English valued by institutions such as schools. In other words, the girls are more likely to see non-standard forms as being inappropriate in the school context, and to style-shift accordingly.

Not all the boys used fewer non-standard verb forms in school (as would be predicted by the Labovian model, with non-standard features reducing as the situation becomes more formal). The boys' speech in school is shown to be linked to their relationship with their teacher. Where they have a good relationship with the teacher, they use fewer non-standard present tense verb forms; that is, they adapt their speech in the direction of school norms. Where they have a poor relationship with their teacher, on the other hand, they either maintain their vernacular usage or actually increase the proportion of non-standard forms in their speech. One of the boys studied by Cheshire used non-standard speech in this way to mark his hostility to the school: he diverged from Standard English more in school than in the adventure playground, presumably to mark his loyalty to the vernacular culture.

Milroy suggests that a status-based model of the kind initially developed by Labov in New York City (and described in 4.2.1) is inadequate to deal with the language patterns of urban populations such as Belfast. She asserts the importance of solidarity as a factor in influencing patterns of language use. The status-based model would predict that speakers who belong to relatively loose-knit networks will change their speech in the direction of publicly legitimised norms (Standard English). However, in Belfast, speakers from the Hammer, with more loose-knit networks resulting from re-housing and unemployment, are *not* more standardised than Ballymacarrett or Clonard speakers. The change in their speech patterns shows a drift away from the focused vernacular norms of more tight-knit groups, but not a drift towards the prestige norms of Standard English. In working class communities, then, it is more accurate to say that men's speech differs from women's because men's tight-knit networks exercise control over their members and maintain vernacular norms. It seems that working class women are not aiming at prestige norms; they belong to relatively loose-knit networks which have less capacity to enforce focused linguistic norms, and they therefore use vernacular forms less consistently than men. This is quite different from claiming that women and men are aiming at different norms.

5.3 WOMEN AS LAMES

In his work on the speech of black adolescent peer groups in New York, Labov introduces the term *lame* to refer to isolated individuals on the fringes of vernacular culture: 'To be lame means to be outside of the central group and its culture' (Labov 1972b:258). Labov demonstrated that lames differ systematically in their use of language from full members of the peer group: while their speech is still very non-standard, it is much less close to the vernacular than is the speech of members of the street culture. For example, if we look at one grammatical feature of the Black English Vernacular – negative concord – we find that the adolescent peer group known as the Thunderbirds uses negative concord 98 per cent of the time, while the lames use it only 76 per cent of the time. For the Thunderbirds it is a semicategorical rule; for the lames it is a variable rule. (Note however that 76 per cent as a score for the use of negative concord is still very high: the lames are certainly not approximating to (white) prestige norms.)

Can we describe women as lames? The work of both Milroy and Cheshire demonstrates that female speakers are less closely integrated into vernacular culture, that female speakers use vernacular norms less consistently than male speakers, and that these two findings are interrelated. In this respect, women are like Labov's lames. But Labov used the term or refer to isolated individuals. Most women are not isolated: among the women in Belfast studied by Milroy only three had a Network Strength Score of 0; among the Reading adolescents, only two of the girls are clearly peripheral (see Fig. 5.6). Women do belong to social networks, but these seem to be less dense and multiplex than those of men.[2]

So in the sense that they are not isolated individuals and do belong to social networks, the term 'lame' is not applicable. However, 'lame' in Labov's work also means an individual characterised by significantly lower usage of vernacular forms. In this sense, female speakers in both Belfast and Reading do seem to be lames.

Our understanding of the language of working-class women is

greatly increased by our understanding of the function of the peer group or social network as a norm-enforcing mechanism. We can see that, because of their low level of integration into networks, women's linguistic usage is distanced from the vernacular. Like Labov's lames, their speech reflects neither the vernacular norms of the peer group, nor the standard norms of the legitimised culture. It hovers between the extremes of the (working-class, male) vernacular and prestigious (middle-class) Standard English. Explanations discussed in Chapter 4 described sex differences in terms of speakers' positive choice of one of two opposing sets of norms. Social network theory reveals that differences may be the result of a *lack* of norms.

5.4 CHANGING PATTERNS: THE YOUNG CLONARD WOMEN

Traditionally it is working-class men who belong to the dense multiplex social networks which are capable of sustaining vernacular norms. Young speakers of both sexes who reject mainstream culture and who conform to peer group pressures (strong for boys, weaker for girls) use vernacular speech to a greater or lesser extent. It is in adulthood that we find the traditional split between male and female speakers resulting from the social patterns so illuminated by Milroy. So in Norwich, Glasgow, West Wirral, and Ballymacarrett in Belfast, we find men using consistently more non-standard speech.

This pattern is not, however, immutable, but merely reflects society. With recession and growing male unemployment, new patterns may emerge. The Clonard community in Belfast shows that, where men lose their interaction patterns and women live as neighbours and work and amuse themselves together, then it is *women* who display consistent usage of vernacular forms.[3] As we saw above (5.1.1), the young Clonard women have the highest Network Strength Score of any sub-group. The strength of their network ties is reflected in the homogeneity of their linguistic forms. The idea that speakers are attracted to vernacular speech because of its connotations of masculinity is clearly an inappropriate explanation of the young Clonard women's speech behaviour. Vernacular speech may have connotations of masculinity because of its traditional association with working-class *male* speakers. However it is important not to confuse effect for cause. The reasons why members of speech communities speak as they do are extremely complex. It is only by examining closely the social processes underlying linguistic behaviour that we can hope to improve our understanding of linguistic usage. This is the aim of sociolinguistics. Social network theory provides a valuable insight into why individual speakers use vernacular forms with greater or less consistency. At the same time, it helps us to understand linguistic differences between male and female speakers.

NOTES

1 The Belfast material is based on Milroy and Milroy 1978; Milroy 1980; Milroy 1982. The Reading material comes from Cheshire 1978; Cheshire 1982a; Cheshire 1982b.

2 Work in other cultures suggests that this is not always the pattern – in her study of Tenejapa (a Mayan community in Mexico), Penelope Brown observes that 'where men dominate the public sphere of life and women stick largely to the domestic sphere, it seems likely that female relationships will be relatively multi-stranded, male ones relatively single-stranded' (Brown 1980:134).

3 It should be noted that the Clonard young women's use of other variables was in line with 'normal' female usage, but Lesley Milroy points out that (a) is a particularly important variable in Belfast and is currently undergoing change (see 8.3.4).

Chapter Six

Sex differences in communicative competence

6.1 THE CONCEPT OF COMMUNICATIVE COMPETENCE

So far I have used the term *language* in the narrow sense of grammar and phonology, the formal structure of language. The sex differences in language described in Chapters 4 and 5 were differences in women's and men's syntax, morphology and pronunciation. This focus on linguistic form, with the sentence as the highest unit of structure, was established in linguistics and has been carried over into sociolinguistics: there are many sociolinguists who consider studies of social variation in grammar and phonology to be 'sociolinguistics proper'. Given the current prestige of linguistics as a discipline, it is not surprising that sociolinguists – especially those whose original training was in linguistics – have accepted the linguistic orthodoxy. It is becoming more and more apparent, however, that this view of language is far too narrow. The sociolinguist has to deal with real language data from a wide variety of situations; anyone who has ever studied conversational interaction will know that they cannot deal adequately with it if they restrict themselves to sentence grammar.

In response to the growing awareness that the study of language should be more than the study of grammar and phonology, new disciplines have emerged such as discourse analysis and pragmatics; while others, such as ethnomethodology and speech act theory, have experienced a revival of interest. The concept which marks the beginning of this revival of interest in language in its broadest sense is **communicative competence**. The term was first used by Dell Hymes (1972). He argued that it was essential to incorporate social and cultural factors into linguistic description. The child, in Chomsky's view, internalises a set of rules which enable her/him to produce grammatical sentences; according to

Hymes, however, the child learns not just grammar but also a sense of **appropriateness**. It is not sufficient for the child to be linguistically competent; in order to function in the real world, s/he must also have learned when to speak, when to remain silent, what to talk about – and how to talk about it – in different circumstances. Imagine someone who speaks at the same time as others, who doesn't repond to questions, who looks away when addressed, who stands embarrassingly close to another speaker, who doesn't laugh when someone tells a joke . . . . Such a person might use well-formed sentences, but we would all recognise that they were *incompetent* in an important sense. It is this knowledge of how language is used in a given society which constitutes communicative competence.

6.2 THE COMMUNICATIVE COMPETENCE OF WOMEN AND MEN

In this chapter I shall look at ways in which women and men seem to differ in terms of their communicative competence. They differ, in other words, in their sense of what is *appropriate* for them as speakers. Much work – some of it contradictory – has been done in this area, though in some cases the evidence is suggestive rather than conclusive.

Sex differences in communicative competence are part of folk knowledge (as we saw in Chapter 2). In Britain, for example, we all grow up to believe that women talk more than men, that women 'gossip', that men swear more than women, that women are more polite, and so on. Research in this area often directly challenges cultural stereotypes, since much of the folklore associated with male/female differences turns out to be false.

In this chapter I shall look first at turn-taking in conversation in some detail, then at certain aspects of female usage which have been labelled 'women's style', then at politeness and its linguistic correlates. I shall examine the question, how far is women's language really powerless language? and the chapter will end with a brief appraisal of linguistic interaction in all-female groups.

6.2.1 Turn-taking in conversation: interruptions and topic control

Any analysis of conversational interaction needs a model of normal conversation structure. The diagram below is a flow chart which represents the way turns are taken in a normal conversation. It is based on Sacks et al's (1974) model of turn-taking in naturally occurring conversation. (The diamonds represent decision points.) The current speaker in conversation may select the next speaker (by asking them a question, for example, or addressing them by name), in which case the person selected must speak next. If the current speaker does not select the next speaker, then one of the other participants in the conversation can opt to speak next. If none of them does so, then the current speaker has the option of continuing to speak.

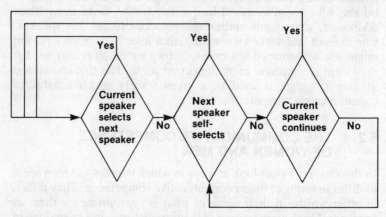

Figure 6.1: Flow chart showing turn-taking in conversation (based on Zimmerman and West 1975:110)

Zimmerman and West (1975) taped thirty-one conversations involving two participants 'in coffee shops, drug stores and other public places' on the campus of the University of California; ten conversations took place between two women, ten between two men, and eleven between one woman and one man. They analysed these conversations in terms of the model shown in Figure 6.1, because they were particularly interested in the mechanisms of turn-taking. How do speakers know when it is their turn to speak? It seems that participants in conversation anticipate the end of the current turn by using syntactic and semantic clues. Evidence for the close syntactic and semantic monitoring we do of others' speech is provided by cases where one speaker contributes to or completes another's turn (so you get either speaker A and B speaking together, or B finishing A's utterance). The following examples, both from spontaneously occurring conversation, illustrate this.

(1)   A: but we've got   four still alive now
        B: four   m
        (Coates 1984a)

(2)   A: the continentals I suppose they came in late and
        B:

```
A:   they build them
B:                    properly
```
(Crystal & Davy 1975:21)

This ability to anticipate the end of a speaker's turn means that one turn follows another very smoothly, often with no pause intervening. (Minimal responses such as *mhm*, *yeah*, or *m* as in example (1) don't constitute a turn: they are a way of indicating the listener's positive attention to the speaker, and thus a way of supporting the speaker in their choice of topic.)

Zimmerman and West examined irregularities in the transcribed conversations, that is, points in the conversations where turn-taking did not follow the smooth pattern described above. They found profound differences between the conversations involving two speakers of the same sex and those involving one speaker of each sex. The two sorts of irregularity they identified are called **overlap** and **interruption**.

Overlaps are instances of slight over-anticipation by the next speaker: instead of beginning to speak immediately following current speaker's turn, next speaker begins to speak at the very end of current speaker's turn, overlapping the last word (or part of it). **Interruptions**, on the other hand, are violations of the turn-taking rules of conversation. Next speaker begins to speak while current speaker is still speaking, at a point in current speaker's turn which could not be defined as the last word. Interruptions break the symmetry of the conversational model: the interruptor prevents the speaker from finishing their turn, at the same time gaining a turn for themselves.

The two tables given below show the number of overlaps and interruptions occurring in the conversations analysed by Zimmerman and West.

Table 6.1: Turn-taking irregularities in twenty same-sex pairs (based on Zimmerman and West 1975:115)

	1st speaker	2nd speaker	Total
Overlaps	12	10	22
Interruptions	3	4	7

Table 6.2: Turn-taking irregularities in eleven mixed-sex pairs (based on Zimmerman and West 1975:116)

	Male speakers	Female speakers	Total
Overlaps	9	0	9
Interruptions	46	2	48

Table 6.1 deals with the conversations which took place between speakers of the same sex (two women or two men). Here, in twenty conversations, there were twenty-two overlaps, divided twelve and ten between the participants, and there were seven interruptions, of which three involved the first speaker and four the second. (For the purposes of the analysis, the person speaking first in a given stretch of conversation was labelled 'first speaker'; this does not mean that this speaker initiated the conversation.)

These results are in complete contrast with those given in Table 6.2, where the conversations involved one member of each sex. In these eleven conversations there were nine overlaps and forty-eight interruptions. All of the overlaps were caused by the male speaker, and forty-six of the forty-eight interruptions were cases of the man interrupting the woman. These results were checked to see that they weren't caused by one abnormal conversation: the interruptions occurred in every conversation except one.

Note that the number of interruptions is very high when we consider that there were only seven in the twenty same-sex conversations. The ratio of interruptions to conversation is 0.35:1 (7 out of 20) for same-sex conversations, and 4.36:1 (48 out of 11) for mixed-sex conversations. Secondly, note that Table 6.1 shows us that men rarely interrupt one another; it is when they are talking to women that they use interruptions. These results indicate that in mixed-sex conversations men infringe women's right to speak, specifically women's right to finish a turn. Conversely, the fact that women used no overlaps in conversation with men (while they did use some in same-sex conversations) suggests that women are concerned *not* to violate the man's turn but to wait until he's finished.

What effects do such violations of normal turn-taking in conversation have? It seems that after overlaps and especially after interruptions, speakers tend to fall silent. Since most interruptions (according to Zimmerman and West's data) are produced by men in mixed-sex conversations, the speaker who falls silent is usually a woman. Silence is often a sign of malfunction in conversation: under ideal conditions, participants in conversation alternate their turns smoothly, with little or no gap between turns. Zimmerman and West found that the average silence in single sex conversations lasted for 1.35 seconds, while the average silence in mixed-sex conversations lasted for 3.21 seconds.

These silences resulted not just from interruptions and overlaps, but also from delayed minimal responses. Minimal responses, such as *mhm* or *yeah*, are a way of indicating the listener's positive attention to the speaker. The listener has an active, not a passive, role in conversation, and minimal responses (as well as paralinguistic features such as smiling, nodding, grimacing) signal active attention. The following extract illustrates this:

(3)   and this put her into a bit of a flap (*m*) so before she could do
        anything about this she had to pull forwards (*m*) in order to er to
        open the gates so she took the car out of reverse, put it into first
        gear (*yeah*) and pulled forward very gently (*yeah*).
        (Crystal & Davy 1975:44)

Zimmerman and West found that in mixed-sex conversations male speakers often delayed their minimal responses. In other words, they said *m* or *yeah* at an appropriate point but only after a pause. It seems that a delayed minimal response may function to signal a lack of understanding or a lack of interest in what the current speaker is saying. Just as a well-placed minimal response demonstrates active attention on the part of the listener and support for the speaker's topic, so a delayed minimal response signals a lack of interest in the speaker's topic.

When talking with women, men seem to use interruptions and delayed minimal responses to deny women the right to control the topic of conversation. Men disobey the normal turn-taking rules (as set out in Fig. 6.1) in order to control topics. Work on adult-child conversations shows a similar pattern, with adults abusing the system in order to control topics. We will look at adult-child conversation in Chapter 7.

Control of topics is normally shared equally between participants in a conversation. In conversations between speakers of the same sex, this seems to be the pattern, but when one speaker is male and one female, male speakers tend to **dominate**. Conversational **dominance** is the focus of research by Leet-Pellegrini (1980) which looks at the interaction of the independent variables sex of speaker and expertise. Expertise refers to the speaker's level of knowledge of the topic under discussion. By examining linguistic features such as talkativeness, interruptions, overlaps and minimal responses, Leet-Pellegrini was able to establish that *in conjunction* the variables of sex and expertise were a good predictor of dominance. In other words, speakers who were both male *and* well-informed tended to dominate conversation. They talked more and infringed the other speaker's turns more. On the other hand, speakers who were both female and uninformed talked less and used more minimal responses and other supportive linguistic behaviour. Male speakers who were well-informed dominated conversation because they used a style of interaction based on power (asserting an unequal right to talk and to control topics) while well-informed female speakers preferred an interactional style based on

101

solidarity and support. These findings will be taken up in 6.4 and 6.5.

Research on the use of minimal responses is unanimous in showing that women use them more and at appropriate moments, that is, at points in conversation which indicate the listener's support for the current speaker (Strodtbeck & Mann 1956; Hirschmann 1974; Fishman 1980; Zimmerman & West 1980). It is also claimed that when women speak, they make their utterances more tentative by using forms – **hedges** – such as *you know, sort of, just*.[1] A statement like *It was – you know – really interesting* is less assertive than the unhedged version. *It was really interesting.* Fishman, who taped the daily conversations of three young American couples (a total of fifty-two hours of speech), found that the women used *you know* five times more than the men in the twelve-and-a-half hours of conversation which she transcribed (women 87: men 17). In interactional terms, *you know* is an attention-getting device: the speaker checks that the addressee is listening and comprehending. It is also often an invitation to the addressee to respond (i.e. it signals the potential end of a turn). When Fishman analysed her transcripts, she found that the *you knows* used by women were clustered at certain points. Thirty of the eighty-seven came in six short segments of talk, where the women were unsuccessfully attempting to pursue topics of conversation. These six segments, containing 35 per cent of the examples of *you know*, constitute less than 2 per cent of the total transcript. The following is a brief example (figures in brackets indicate length of pause in seconds):

(4)   in other words black women are white (2) *y'know* it's really a
       simplistic article (0.5) *you know* he starts off saying – this – (1)
       y'know (0.8) sort of this gross indiscriminate black versus white
       (1) vision and . . . (Fishman 1980:130)

Note how the *you knows* occur immediately before or after pauses, at points where the woman expects (but doesn't get) some response from the man. *You know* reveals malfunction in turn-taking: change of speaker is not occurring because the man is not participating in the conversation (he rejects the topic under discussion). The use of *you know* by women in mixed-sex conversation is evidence of the work they have to do to try to keep conversation going. Women use *you know* more than men because it is men rather than women who fail to respond minimally or with a full turn at appropriate points. (In the cases where Fishman *did* find men using *you know*, it was doing the same work.)

6.2.2 'Women's style'

The claim that women and men typically employ different

linguistic 'styles' is followed up in a wide range of studies. I shall summarise some of these in this section, under the headings Verbosity, Tag questions, Questions, Commands and directives, Swearing and taboo language.

Verbosity

There is a widespread belief in our society that women talk more than men, yet research findings consistently contradict this. Men have been shown to talk more than women in settings as diverse as staff meetings (Eakins & Eakins 1978), television panel discussions (Bernard 1972), experimental pairs (Argyle et al. 1968), and also husband-and-wife pairs in spontaneous conversation (Soskin & John 1963). When asked to describe three pictures, male subjects took on average 13.00 minutes per picture compared with 3.17 minutes for female subjects (Swacker 1975). As we have seen (2.2.6), Spender (1980a) explains the persistence of this myth of the talkative women by suggesting that we have different expectations of male and female speakers: while men have the right to talk, women are expected to remain silent – talking at any length, then, will be perceived as talkativeness in women.

The word *chatter*, which is nearly always used of women rather than men, has two main semantic components: verbosity and triviality. The idea that women discuss topics which are essentially trivial has probably contributed to the myth of women's verbosity, since talk on trivial topics can more easily be labelled 'too much'. The evidence is that women and men *do* tend to discuss different topics (see Aries 1976; Haas 1979; Stone 1983), as do girls and boys (this will be discussed in Chapter 7). However, the fact that topics such as sport, politics, cars are seen as 'serious' while topics such as child-rearing and personal relationships are labelled 'trivial' is simply a reflection of social values which define what men do as important, and conversely what women do as less important.

Tag questions

Lakoff (1975) suggested that women are perceived as expressing themselves in a more tentative way than men. She nominated the tag question as one of the linguistic forms associated with tentativeness, but provided no empirical evidence to show that women use more tag questions than men.

According to Lakoff, tag questions decrease the strength of assertions. Compare the two sentences below:

(5a)   The crisis in the Middle East is terrible.

(5b)   The crisis in the Middle East is terrible, isn't it?

Lakoff claims that women use sentences like (5b), which contains the tag question *isn't it*, more often than men, who are supposed to

103

favour (5a). Siegler and Siegler (1976) presented students with sixteen sentences, four of which were assertions with tag questions, like (5b) above. The students were told that the sentences came from conversations between college students, and were asked to guess whether a woman or a man produced the sentence originally. The results of this test supported Lakoff's hypothesis: sentences with tag questions were most often attributed to women, while strong assertions, like (5a), were most often attributed to men (the difference in attributions was statistically significant). This however only confirms what speakers' *attitudes* are; it doesn't prove that women actually use more tag questions.

While several studies have confirmed that English speakers *assume* a connection between tag questions and female linguistic usage (see O'Barr and Atkins 1980; Jones 1980, to be discussed in 6.4 and 6.5 respectively), one of the rare studies which set out to test this assumption empirically found it unproven. Dubois & Crouch (1975)) used as their data the discussion sessions following various formal papers given at a day conference. They listed all examples of formal tag questions (such as 'Probably industrial too, isn't it?') as well as 'informal' tags (such as 'Right?', 'OK?' as in 'That's not too easy, right?'). A total of thirty-three tag questions was recorded (seventeen formal and sixteen informal), and these were *all* produced by men.[2]

All this work is based on the questionable assumption that there is a one-to-one relationship between linguistic form (tag question) and extra-linguistic factor (tentativeness) (see Cameron 1985:55 for a discussion of this point). Refreshingly, Holmes (1984) analyses tags according to whether they express primarily **modal** or **affective** meaning. Tags with primaily **modal** meaning signal the speaker's degree of certainty about the proposition expressed:

(6) She's coming around noon   (*Husband to wife concerning*
     isn't she   *expected guest*)

Such tags can be described as **speaker-oriented** since they ask the addressee to confirm the speaker's proposition. Tags whose primary function is **affective** express the speaker's attitude to the addressee (and are therefore **addressee-oriented**). They do this either by supporting the addressee (facilitative tags):

(7) The hen's brown isn't she   (*Teacher to pupil*)

or by softening the force of negatively affective speech acts:

(8) That was pretty silly wasn't it   (*Older child to younger friend*)

Table 6.3 shows the overall distribution of tags in a corpus consisting of equal amounts of female and male speech in matched

Table 6.3 Distribution of tag questions according to sex of speaker and function of tag in discourse (Holmes 1984:54)

Type of meaning	No. of tag questions F	M
Modal meaning: degree of certainty. Speaker-oriented tags signalling speaker's degree of certainty about proposition: e.g. requesting reassurance, confirmation, agreement etc.	18 (35%)	24 (61%)
Affective meaning Addressee-oriented tags		
(1) Facilitative Expressing speaker's solidarity with or positive attitude to addressee: e.g. facilitating speaker's contribution to discourse	30 (59%)	10 (25%)
(2) Softening Expressing politeness or speaker's concern for addressee's feelings, e.g. softening force of criticism, directive etc.	3 (6%)	5 (13%)
	51	39

contexts. Women and men do not differ greatly in total usage (but note that women do turn out to use more tags). However, the important point to notice is that 59 per cent of the tags used by women are facilitative (compared with 25 per cent for men) while 61 per cent of the tags used by men are modal, expressing uncertainty (compared with 35 per cent for women).

When the relationship between the participants in the interaction is taken into account, it emerges that **facilitators** are more likely to use tags than non-facilitators (Holmes uses the term *facilitator* to refer to those responsible for ensuring that interaction proceeds smoothly, e.g. interviewers on radio and television, discussion group leaders, teachers, hosts). Moreover, women are more likely than men to use tags when acting as facilitators. The significance of Holmes's findings will be taken up in the discussion of women and politeness (6.3) and of women and powerless language (6.4).

Questions

Fishman (1980) analysed her transcripts of couples in conversation for questions as well as for *you know*. She looked at yes/no questions such as 'Did you see Sarah last night?' as well as at tag questions. The women in her sample used three times as many tag and yes/no questions as the men (87 : 29). During the twelve-and-a-half hours of conversation transcribed, a total of 370 questions was asked, of which women asked 263 (two-and-a-half times as many as the men). A survey of the linguistic behaviour of people buying a ticket at Central Station in Amsterdam also established that women ask more questions than men, especially when addressing a *male* ticket-seller (Brouwer et al. 1979). Why should this be so? Are men seen as repositories of knowledge, and women as ignorant? Perhaps women feel less inhibited about asking for information, since this does not conflict with the sex-role prescribed by society.

Fishman prefers to explain women's question-asking in linguistic terms. Questions are part of the conversational sequencing device Question + Answer. Questions and answers are linked together in conversation: questions demand a response from the addressee. In interactive terms, then, questions are stronger than statements, since they give the speaker the power to elicit a response. As we saw in the model of turn-taking in conversation presented in Fig. 6.1, current speaker can exercise the option to select next speaker. Example (9) below demonstrates that tag quesions are also used to elicit a response (a minimal response rather than a full turn):

(9) A: Three and six a week I used to get – and me Mum used to give me money on top of that to keep me out of trouble didn't she
B: yes.
me Mum used to always give me a couple of bob
B: yeah (Coates, Birkenhead survey, 1983)

Speaker A uses the tag *didn't she* to nudge B into an active role. In the following extract (taken from Pinter's *The Birthday Party*) note how Petey is forced into conversation by Meg's use of questions:

(10) (*Meg gives Petey a bowl of cornflakes. He sits at the table, props up his paper and starts to eat*)
Meg: Are they nice?
Petey: Very nice.
Meg: I thought they'd be nice. You got your paper?
Petey: Yes.
Meg: Is it good?
Petey: Not bad.
Meg: What does it say?
Petey: Nothing much.

Research findings so far suggest that women use interrogative forms more than men and that this may reflect women's relative weakness in interactive situations: they exploit questions and tag questions in order to keep conversation going.

Commands and directives

We can define a directive as a speech act which tries to get someone to do something. Goodwin (1980) observed the group play of girls and boys in a Philadelphia street, and noticed that the boys used different sorts of directives from the girls. The boys used explicit commands:

(11) *Michael: Gimme* the pliers (*Poochie gives pliers to Michael*)

(12) *Huey: Get off* my steps (*Poochie moves down steps*)

Michael, the leader of the group, often supported his commands with statements of his own desires:

(13) *Michael:* Gimme the wire . . . Look man, I want the wire cutters right now.

The girls, by contrast, typically used directives such as the following:

(14) *Terry:* Hey y'all let's use these first and then come back and get the rest cuz it's too many of 'em.

(15) *Sharon:* Let's go around Subs and Suds.
      Pam: Let's ask her 'Do you have any bottles?'

The form *let's* is hardly ever used by the boys: it explicitly includes the speaker in the proposed action. The girls' use *of gonna* (see 16 below) exploits suggestions for future action as a form of directive:

(16) *Sharon:* We *gonna* paint 'em and stuff.

The modal auxiliaries *can* and *could* are also used by the girls to suggest rather than demand action:

(17) *Pam:* We *could* go around looking for more bottles.

(18) *Sharon:* Hey maybe tomorrow we *can* come up here and see if they got some more.

Note the use of the adverbial *maybe* in (18) to further soften the directive.

While Goodwin demonstrates convincingly that the girls and boys use quite different linguistic means to express directives when playing in same-sex groups, she stresses that this does not mean that girls are incapable of using more forceful directives in other contexts (such as in cross-sex arguments). She argues that the linguistic forms used reflect the social organisation of the group: the boys' group is hierarchically organised, with leaders using very strong directive forms to demonstrate control, while the girls' group is non-hierarchical with all girls participating in decision-making on an equal basis.

Engle's (1980b) study of the language of parents when they play with their children revealed that fathers tend to give directions:

(19)   Why don't you make a chimney?

(20)   Off! Take it off!

Mothers, on the other hand, are more likely to consult the child's wishes:

(21)   Do you want to look at any of the other toys over here?

(22)   What else shall we put on the truck?

Not only were the fathers more directive than the mothers, they were more directive with their sons than with their daughters. These linguistic differences again reflect a difference in organisation: mothers view interaction as an occasion to help children learn how to choose: fathers were less concerned with the children's desires and introduced new ideas. Differences in parents' speech to children will be taken up in Chapter 7.

Swearing and taboo language

There is little hard evidence on male/female differences in swearing, though as we saw in Chapter 2 the folklinguistic belief that men swear more than women and use more taboo words is widespread. Jespersen claimed in 1922 (see 2.2.2) that women have an 'instinctive shrinking from coarse and gross expressions and a preference for refined and (in certain spheres) veiled and indirect expressions'. In his preface to the *Dictionary of American Slang*, Flexner claims that 'most American slang is created and used by males' (Flexner 1960:xii). Lakoff (1975) also claims that men use stronger expletives (*damn*, *shit*) than women (*oh dear*, *goodness*), but her evidence is purely impressionistic.

Kramer (1974) analysed cartoons from *The New Yorker*. She found that cartoonists make their male characters swear much more freely than the female characters. She asked students to identify captions taken from the cartoons as male or female. For most of the captions there was a clear consensus (at least 66 per cent agreement) on the sex of the speaker, and the students commented explicitly on the way in which swearing distinguished male speech from female speech. A second study (Kramer 1975) used cartoons from four different magazines (*The New Yorker*, *Playboy*, *Cosmopolitan*, *Ladies Home Journal*). Students correctly identified the sex of the speaker in 79 per cent of cases. Analysis of the captions showed that, among other things, women used fewer swear words. Both these studies confirm the existence of a cultural stereotype but provide no evidence as to whether or not men actually *do* swear more than women.

The comments of contemporary sociolinguists on this area of

linguistic usage are unsupported by data. Labov (1971:207) says: 'In middle-class groups, women generally show much less familiarity with and much less tolerance for non-standard grammar and taboo'. Cheshire (1982a:101) selects swearing as one of the measures to be included in her Vernacular Culture Index (see 5.1.2), since, as she says, 'this was a major symbol of vernacular identity for both boys and girls.' This index was applied only to the boys in her sample (since the girls were said not to have a clearly defined system of cultural values) and there is therefore no comparative data.

Gomm (1981) recorded fourteen conversations between young British speakers: the participants were all female in five of these, all male in five, and mixed in four. An analysis of the transcripts of these conversations reveals no qualitative difference in the use of swear words, but Table 6.4 shows the difference in frequency between male and female usage.

Table 6.4: Incidence of swearing in single sex and mixed groups (based on Gomm 1981)

	Single sex groups	Mixed groups	Total
Men	21	4	25
Women	7	2	9

Clearly, the male speakers in Gomm's sample swear more often than the female speakers. Moreover, both women and men swear more in the company of their own sex; male usage of swear words in particular drops dramatically in mixed sex conversations.

6.3 POLITENESS

It is part of folklinguistics, and has also been asserted by linguists, that women are more polite than men. In order to examine this claim, we need to look at what politeness is, and how it is realised linguistically in different societies.

Brown and Levinson (1978) define politeness in terms of the concept of **face**. This term is taken from its everyday usage in phrases like *to lose face*, and respecting face is defined as showing consideration for people's feelings. We show consideration by respecting two basic human needs: (1) the need not to be imposed on (this is called **negative face**); and (2) the need to be liked and admired (this is called **positive face**). In British society, we try to satisfy the **negative face wants** of others by, for example, accompanying requests with apologies for the imposition: 'I'm awfully sorry to bother you but I've run out of milk – could you possibly lend

109

me half a pint?' A request phrased like this makes it possible for the addressee to avoid co-operating. We try to satisfy the **positive face wants** of others by greeting them when we see them, asking them how they are, expressing admiration and approval for what they've been doing and for what they feel about things: 'You're looking marvellous!'; 'I know exactly how you feel'. To ask for something baldly, e.g. 'Give me some milk', or to ignore someone we know in any social setting, is to act impolitely in our society. Politeness, then, can be defined as satisfying the face wants of others, and linguistically this can be carried out in many different ways.

Brown studied the language of women and men in a Mayan community in Mexico, to test the hypothesis that women are more polite than men (Brown 1980). She argues that the level of politeness appropriate to a given interaction will depend on the social relationship of the participants. This means that linguistic markers of politeness are a good indication of social relationships. If women *do* use more polite forms than men, what does this indicate? That women treat men as socially superior? That women treat men as socially distant? That women are involved in more face-threatening acts (that is, that for various reasons, when women address men, their requests etc. impose on men's negative or positive face)?

In Tzeltal, the language spoken by the Mayans, there is a class of particles which operate as adverbials and modify the force of the speech act. To put it simply, they either strengthen or weaken the force of what is said; either *I emphatically/sincerely/really assert/request/promise* . . . or *I tentatively/maybe/perhaps assert/ request/promise* . . . In all languages, you can emphasise the force of your speech act to be positively polite, or hedge the force of your speech act to be negatively polite. In English, for example, the modal auxiliaries *may*, *might* and *could* and the modal adverbs *perhaps*, *possibly*, *maybe*, can be used as hedges by speakers, and thus function as negative politeness strategies. According to Holmes (1984), it is when modals are used to express affective meaning that they show concern for the face needs of others, and are thus politeness markers. Examples (17) and (18) above (p. 107) illustrate such usage.

Brown tested three hypotheses: (1) Women use more strengthening particles when speaking to women (that is, pay a lot of attention to women's positive face wants); (2) women use more weakening particles when speaking to men (that is, pay a lot of attention to men's negative face wants); (3) women speaking to women use more particles than men speaking to men. She compared the speech of male and female speakers in mixed and single-sex pairs, matched as far as possible (her data was spontaneous conversation) for familiarity of participants, status of participants, and speaker's knowledge of the topic (all speakers hedge more when they know less about a topic). The analysis of particles used by members of same-sex pairs showed that Brown's third hypothesis was confirmed: women do use more particles.

Table 6.5 Average number of particles for 100 speech acts in same-sex pairs (based on Brown 1980:122)

	Strengtheners	Weakeners	Total particles
Mean for female pairs	25.2	34.1	59.3
Mean for male pairs	14.4	18.1	32.6

However, her data did not confirm her other two hypotheses, as Table 6.6 (for mixed-sex pairs) shows:

Table 6.6 Average number of particles for 100 speech acts in mixed-sex pairs (based on Brown 1980:123)

	Strengtheners	Weakeners	Total particles
Mean for women speaking to men	35.7	24.4	60.2
Mean for men speaking to women	24.1	33.1	57.2

These tables show us that the women did not use more strengthening particles when speaking to women; in fact, they used more when speaking to men (35.7:25.2). Nor did women use more weakening particles when speaking to men; a comparison of the two tables shows, on the contrary, that women used more weakening particles when speaking to other women (34.1 : 24.4). Why is this?

Brown attempts to explain these results by arguing that conversation between two men in her Mayan community differs in terms of topic so much from conversation between two women that they are not strictly comparable. She emphasises, however, that on the crude measure of gross use of particles women clearly use more, and thus particle-usage in this community is a crude index of politeness. It emerges, as expected, that women are more polite than men.

It seems to me that the most interesting fact thrown up by Tables 6.5 and 6.6 is the particle usage of men talking to men. The averages, in terms of total particles used, are not strikingly dissimilar for the other three possible combinations (men to women, women to women, women to men). In other words, men use a different style with each other, a style characterised by low particle usage; this style differs from that used when they talk to women, or when women talk to women, or when women talk to men.

Brown examined particle usage in Tzeltal to establish what was the full range of expression available to the individual speaker. She came to the conclusion that the usage of women and men differs systematically. Women seem to be alert to the fact that what they are saying may threaten face. This sensitivity to the face needs of others results in different linguistic usage. Women use the extremes of positive and negative politeness; men's speech is more matter-of-fact. Moreover, certain usages – such as the women's use of the diminutive [ʔala], or the men's use of the strengthening particle [melel] in public speaking – result in recognisable 'feminine' and 'masculine' styles.

6.4   POWERFUL AND POWERLESS LANGUAGE

Brown argues that negative politeness – where the speaker apologises for intruding, uses impersonal structures (such as passives), and hedges assertions – is found where people are in an inferior position in society. This deduction is also made by O'Barr and Atkins (1980) in their study of courtroom language. O'Barr and Atkins observed that manuals for lawyers on tactics in court often treated female witnesses as a special case. This led them to wonder if female witnesses differed *linguistically* from male witnesses. They analysed transcrips of 150 hours of trials in a North Carolina superior criminal court, looking at features which they call Women's Language or WL (and which are largely based on Lakoff (1975)). These ten features are listed below.

1. Hedges e.g. *sort of, kind of, I guess*;
2. (Super) polite forms e.g. *would you please . . . I'd really appreciate it if . . .* ;
3. Tag questions[3];
4. Speaking in italics, e.g. emphatic *so* and *very*, intonational emphasis equivalent to underlining words in written language;
5. Empty adjectives, e.g. *divine, charming, sweet, adorable*;
6. Hypercorrect grammar and pronunciation;

7. Lack of a sense of humour e.g. poor at telling jokes;

8. Direct quotations;

9. Special vocabulary, e.g. specialised colour terms;

10. Question intonation in declarative contexts.

Each witness was given a score arrived at by dividing the total number of WL features used by the number of utterances. Scores varied from 1.39 (indicating an average of more than one WL feature per utterance) to 0.18 (indicating very infrequent use of WL features). The following is an example of speech high in WL features:

(23)　*Lawyer:* What was the nature of your acquaintance with the late Mrs. E.D.?

　　　Witness A: Well, we were, uh, very close friends. Uh, she was even sort of like a mother to me.

This witness gained an overall score of 1.14. The following is an example of speech low in WL features:

(24)　*Lawyer:* And had the heart not been functioning, in other words, had the heart been stopped, there would have been no blood to have come from that region?

　　　Witness C: It may leak down depending on the position of the body after death. But the presence of blood in the alveoli indicates that some active respiratory action had to take place.

Witness C gained an overall score of 0.18.

Both these examples are taken from the speech of *female* witnesses, and they show that the use of WL features (as defined by O'Barr and Atkins for this study) does not correlate with sex of speaker. They found that not only did some female witnesses use very few WL features, but also that some male witnesses used a high proportion of WL features. The example below comes from the speech of witness D, a man:

(25)　*Lawyer:* And you saw, you observed what?

　　　Witness D: Well, after I heard – I can't really, I can't definitely state whether the brakes or the lights came first, but I rotated my head slightly to the right, and looked directly behind Mr Z, and I saw reflections of lights, and uh, very, very, very instantaneously after that, I heard a very, very, very loud explosion – from my standpoint of view it would have been an implosion because everything was forced outward like this, like a grenade thrown into a room. And, uh, it was, it was terrifically loud.

Witness D's score for WL features was 1.39 – higher than that of witness A.

O'Barr and Atkins' findings can be summarised as follows:

1. WL features are not characteristic of the speech of all women (see for example witness C).

2. WL features are not restricted to the speech of female speakers (see for example witness D).

3. The scores of speakers can be placed on a continuum (from high to low) – more women have high scores while more men have low scores.

O'Barr and Atkins argue that Lakoff's description of such features as 'Women's Language' is inaccurate. They show that the frequency of WL features in the speech of the witnesses in their study correlates not with sex, but with two other factors – firstly, with the speaker's social status, and secondly with the speaker's previous courtroom experience. Witness C is a pathologist who often has to appear in court as an expert witness; she is a highly educated, professional woman. Her low score for WL features correlates with her high social status and her courtroom experience. Witnesses A and D, on the other hand, who both have high scores, have low social status and little courtroom experience (A is a housewife; D is an inexperienced ambulance attendant).

On the basis of this correlation, O'Barr and Atkins rename the linguistic features normally associated with women's speech **Powerless Language**. They argue that powerless language has been confused with women's language because, in societies like ours, women are usually less powerful than men. Many women therefore typically use powerless language, but this is the result of their position in society rather than of their sex. While powerless and powerful language often correlate with female and male speakers, it is important that sociolinguists and others concerned to explore male/female differences in language keep the non-linguistic variables of sex and social status apart.

6.5 WOMEN TALKING TO WOMEN

Interest is growing in the use of language in all-female groups. 'Gossip' is a term used almost exclusively of women's talk; it usually has pejorative connotations ('idle talk . . . tittle-tattle', *Concise Oxford Dictionary*). Jones (1980) accepts it as a term describing women's talk, but re-defines it in a non-pejorative way as 'a way of talking between women in their roles as women, intimate in style, personal and domestic in topic and setting'. Using a term such as *gossip* draws attention to the fact that the language women use when talking to each other has not traditionally been treated as serious linguistic data; by contrast, men's talk is seen as 'real' talk and has always been taken seriously.

Jones' use of the term *gossip* is not original: it is used in anthropological work to refer to informal communication between members of a social group. Anthropologists stress, among other things, the social function of gossip – it maintains 'the unity, morals and values of social groups' (Gluckman, as quoted in Jones 1980). This is clearly an important function.

Using the sociolinguistic framework established by Ervin-Tripp (1972), Jones describes gossip in terms of the relations between setting, participants, topic, formal features and functions. The setting for women's talk is typically the home, and also sometimes shops, supermarkets, hairdressers. The home is a setting which can be labelled private rather than public. The participants are, self-evidently, women. The topics stem from women's chief roles as wife, mother and housewife, and thus range from husbands and child-rearing to housework. Clearly, discussion of such topics can vary widely, from a simple exchange of recipes to an intense interaction involving women in mutual self-disclosure.

In terms of formal features, Jones describes gossip along the lines already discussed in this and previous chapters: gossip is said to be characterised by the use of questions and tag questions, rising intonation patterns, minimal responses such as *mhm* and *yeah*, paralinguistic responses (raised eyebrows, pursed lips, sighs, etc.) and in general by a reciprocal pattern of interaction.

Her most significant observation is that, where men disagree with or ignore each others' utterances, women tend to acknowledge and build on them. In other words, it seems that men pursue a style of interaction based on **power**, while women pursue a style based on **solidarity** and **support**. At a purely descriptive level, Stone's (1983) account of how he, a man who chose to stay at home and look after his children, experienced women's mode of discourse confirms Jones' work. He describes men's talk as follows:

> From football to sex, from politics to literature, talk had one thing in common; it knew where it was going. It wasn't baffled, it wasn't awed, it wasn't speculative . . . as a rule these conversations were gladiatorial, a contest in language with a familiar topic the arena.

He goes on: 'while I still miss the stimulation of battling wit against wit I am beginning to be satisfied by a different sort of language'. He then sketches a description of this different sort of language, that is, women's language:

What do we talk about? It's obvious. We talk about ailments, bowel and bladder functions and household chores. . . . Most of all we talk about children . . . expressed in short and perfunctory statements that are accommodated with humour and concern by people whose common experience lends an intimacy to their understanding . . . . The constant care of children imbues those involved with . . . a need *to cooperate rather than compete*, . . . a willingness to accept confusion and speculation as an end rather than rely on the dogma of formulae. (my italics)

Kalcik (1975), who studied personal narrative in all-women groups, also argues that the prime pattern of interaction in such groups is co-operative rather than competitive, and this is confirmed by Aries's (1976) work on mixed and single-sex groups. Aries analysed the interaction patterns of six experimental groups: two all-female, two all-male, and two mixed. The all-male groups were concerned to establish where each member stood in relation to other members and in these groups a hierarchy emerged with some members holding dominant positions and others more submissive positions. The two women's groups, on the other hand, were more flexible: active speakers were concerned to draw out more reticent speakers and the women developed ways to express affection and interpersonal concern.

The work referred to in this section is all based on white, middle-class speakers. However, Goodwin's work on the street play of black children in Philadelphia (described in 6.2.2) established that the linguistic forms used by the children reflected the social organisation of their social groups: the non-hierarchical nature of the girls' group resulted in the use of co-operative rather than competitive forms. Wodak (1981) also included working-class speakers in her work on the discourse strategies of women and men in group therapy. She noted interesting class differences: in particular, working-class *men* are considerably more emotional than many middle-class *women*, and working-class speakers in general differ significantly from lower middle-class speakers and from middle-class *men* in their presentation of their problems. However, she also noted significant sex differences. The men and women talked about their problems in different ways: the men tended to use circumstantial descriptions while the women were more personal.

It is to be hoped that future research will pay more attention to the discourse patterns of women talking to women, since it would be valuable to know more about how women's co-operative discourse strategies work. Clearly there are occasions when a co-operative style of interaction will be more appropriate than a competitive style: the ideal (androgynous) speaker would be competent in both.

6.6   CONCLUSION

In this chapter we have looked at work which reveals sex differences in communicative competence. The evidence at present suggests that women and men do pursue different interactive styles: in mixed-sex conversations this means that men tend to interrupt women; they use this strategy to control topics of conversation and their interruptions tend to induce silence in women. Women make greater use of minimal responses to indicate support for the speaker. It also seems that women ask more questions, while men talk more, swear more and use imperative forms to get things done. Women use more linguistic forms associated with politeness. These clusters of linguistic characteristics are sometimes termed 'men's style' and 'women's style'. This terminology is disputed by O'Barr and Atkins who claim that the linguistic features found in the speech of many women are typical of people of low status in society, both women and men, and should more accurately be called 'powerless language'.

This same cluster of linguistic features is shown in a more positive light when examined in the context of women talking to other women. In women-to-women interaction, these 'powerless' forms can be used as a powerful sign of mutual support and solidarity. When used reciprocally, then, it seems that 'powerless' language approaches the ideal form of co-operative discourse – what those who work in the counselling professions call 'co-counselling'. However, the differences between the competitive, assertive male style and the co-operative, supportive female style mean that men will tend to dominate in mixed-sex interaction. (Note that some dissatisfaction with the male style is implied by Aries's finding that the men she studied became less and less interested in attending the all-male sessions and looked forward to the meetings of the mixed groups; the women, on the other hand, preferred the all-women sessions.)

Labov defined the speech community in terms of 'participation in a set of shared norms' (Labov 1972:121). It seems that women and men have different sets of norms for conversational interaction, and we have already seen (in Chapters 4 and 5) that we cannot assume that male and female speakers share grammatical and phonological norms. It seems, then, that women and men constitute distinct speech communities. In the final section of this book, we shall see how this comes about, and examine the linguistic and social consequences of such a distinction.

NOTES

1 Bent Preisler's (unpublished) research into linguistic tentativeness and its correlation with sex roles (which I read too late to incorporate in this book) has shown that women use significantly more hedges than men. His sample contained equal numbers of women and men, from two different age groups (20–25 and 45–50) and from three occupational groups; all the informants lived and worked in Lancaster.
2 Preisler's research (see Note 1) reveals that tag questions, *in combination with* other linguistic forms (e.g. certain modals and other stressed auxiliaries) were used significantly more by women than by men.
3 It should be noted that Holmes' (1984) analysis of spoken interaction shows that tag questions tend to occur more frequently in the speech of facilitators or leaders than in the speech of other participants. This obviously challenges O'Barr and Atkins' claim that tags characterise the speech of the powerless.

Part Three
Causes and Consequences

Chapter Seven

The acquisition of sex-differentiated language

7.1   CHILDREN AND GENDER IDENTITY

The last three chapters have established that women and men differ linguistically in a wide variety of ways. In this chapter I shall look at the way these different repertoires are acquired. Work on child language acquisition is relatively recent, and it tends to concentrate on how the (undifferentiated) child acquires his (sic) language. Language is often interpreted in the narrow sense of grammar, phonology, and lexicon, with particular emphasis on the development of syntax. Classic studies in this field are Bloom (1975), Brown (1976), Dale (1976). More recently, with increased awareness of language as social behaviour, researchers have widened the scope of their enquiries. They still aim to discover how a child becomes linguistically competent, but 'linguistically competent' has been redefined. As was pointed out in Chapter 6, a knowledge of grammar, phonology and lexicon is not enough – it does not make the child competent; children need to master not only the formal rules of language, but also rules for the appropriate use of language. Linguistic competence is now taken to include a knowlege of the cultural norms of spoken interaction. The best work using this new framework is Ochs and Schieffelin's (1983) study of children's acquisition of conversational competence.

Works such as the latter are based on the premise that learning to speak is learning to be a member of a particular culture. The social order, in other words, is reproduced through speech. This being so, and since it seems to be common to all cultures that women's and men's roles are distinguished, it is reasonable to assume that when children learn to speak, one of the things they learn is the cultural role assigned to them on the basis of their sex. This is a two-way process: in becoming linguistically competent, the child learns to be a fully fledged male or female member of the speech community; conversely, when children adopt linguistic behaviour considered appropriate to their sex, they perpetuate the social order which creates gender distinctions.

In Chapter 1 we discussed women and men as social groups, and argued that, despite their greater numbers, women constitute a minority group (see 1.3 and 1.4). Girls and boys learn during childhood to identify with one group or the other. They demonstrate their membership of the group by their use of sex-appropriate behaviour, and this includes sex-appropriate *linguistic* behaviour. Social psychologists refer to this process of learning how to be a 'proper' girl or a 'proper' boy as the acquisition of **gender identity**. In this chapter I shall describe work which demonstrates that sex differences are found in the speech of children. This work is of two kinds. Firstly, there is work which aims to test the belief that girls acquire language at a faster rate than boys; this work will be described briefly. Secondly, there is work which explores children's acquisition of sex-differentiated language in terms of both formal features and communicative competence; this work will be described in some detail. In this second group I shall include work which analyses the ways in which adults – particularly parents – interact with children.

7.2 SEX DIFFERENCES IN EARLY LANGUAGE LEARNING

One of the most well-known and best established generalisations in the area of sex differences is girls' superiority over boys in the acquisition of speech. On measures such as the onset of babbling, the first word, number of words used at 18 months, girls tend to do better than boys. This contrast between girls and boys seems to have been exaggerated in the past, though it has been suggested that differences between male and female children might be diminishing as a reflection of less polarised sex roles and less sexist modes of child care in contemporary societies. However, Maccoby and Jacklin's (1974) authoritative survey of all extant research in the area concluded that the generalisation still holds good. For pre-school children, the research findings indicate that where a sex difference is found, it is nearly always girls who are ahead. Not all these differences achieved statistical significance, but the combined results of all the studies amount to a significant trend. For the early school years, on the other hand, no consistent differences emerge from the research literature, but from the age of 10 or 11, girls again outscore boys on a variety of measures of verbal competence. Some examples of these findings are described below.

Clarke-Stewart (1973) observed American mothers and first-born children for 9 months, from when the children were 9 months until they were 18 months. She found that the language skills of girls in the sample in terms of both comprehension and vocabulary were significantly higher than those of boys; this was paralleled by the girls' more positive involvement with the mother. The girls' mothers differed from the boys' mothers in that they spent more time in the same room as their daughters, had more eye contact with them, used a higher proportion of directive and restrictive behaviours, and a higher ratio of social to referential speech. (Social speech includes greetings, *thank you*, apologies, etc. while referential speech, as its name implies, means speech which refers to things: *What's this?*; *Give me the red brick*, etc.)

Nelson (1973) studied the acquisition of vocabulary by eighteen children between 1 and 2 years of age (again in the U.S.). She divided her sample into two groups according to the rate at which they acquired vocabulary (the index was the age at which the child had acquired fifty words). All the boys fell into the group with a slower acquisition rate. The mean age for fifty words was 18.0 months for the girls and 22.1 months for the boys.

Perkins (1983) reports a study of modal expressions (*can, will, have to, probably*, etc.) used in spontaneous speech by children aged between 6 and 12. His subjects were the ninety-six children taking part in the Polytechnic of Wales Language Development project. All the children were monolingual English speakers, and the sample was balanced in terms of age, sex, and social class. Figure 7.1 (over the page) shows how frequency of use of modal expressions varies in relation to the sex of the child. While the difference between girls and boys is small (not statistically significant), it is girls yet again who are ahead. Interestingly, Perkins found that social class was significantly correlated with modal usage: children from middle-class homes used modal expressions more frequently. This parallelism between girls and the middle-class on one hand and boys and the working-class on the other is something that has been noted earlier (see 4.3.3). In fact, linguistic sex differences seem to be more marked in poorer families: two studies of disadvantaged children (Shipman 1971; Stanford Research Institute 1972) found girls clearly ahead on a number of language measures.

These studies are representative of the many that have been carried out on child language and show a general pattern of girls acquiring language faster than boys. This means that at any given age, girls will be found to be superior in terms of comprehension, size of vocabulary, reading ability, handling of complex expressions such as the modals, etc. While such findings are of interest,

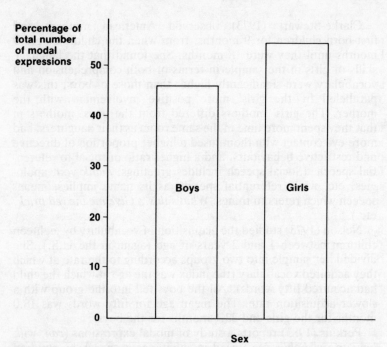

Figure 7.1: The relation of frequency of modal expressions to sex (Perkins 1983:142)

they are not necessarily relevant to the linguistic differences we find between adult speakers of different sexes (many just reflect slower maturation). In the next section, I shall describe work which, it can be argued, shows children developing sex-differentiated language. The linguistic differences described below show girls and boys acquiring the gender-roles prescribed by society.

7.3 THE DEVELOPMENT OF SEX-APPROPRIATE SPEECH

In this section I shall look first at work which describes sex differences in children's language which anticipate formal differences in adult language of the kind described in Chapters 4 and 5; and secondly at work where children's language usage anticipates adult communicative competence differences of the kind described in Chapter 6.

7.3.1 Formal differences

Before puberty, children's vocal tracts differ only in relation to the child's size and not in relation to the child's sex. But work on *pitch* has revealed that sex differences emerge before the onset of puberty. Liebermann's (1967) study suggests that, even before they can talk, babies alter the pitch of their voices depending on the sex of the addressee: their average fundamental frequency is lower when they 'talk' to their fathers than when they 'talk' to their mothers.

Several projects (e.g. Sachs et al. 1973; Meditch 1975; Fichtelius et al. 1980) have tested the ability of adult judges to identify the sex of a child from recorded samples of speech. These projects find that judges identify children correctly as male or female at well above chance level. Further analysis of the child speech samples suggests that it is **formant** patterns which identify speakers as male or female. (A formant is a concentration of acoustic energy, reflecting the way air vibrates in the vocal tract as it changes its shape; most sounds can be described on the basis of three main formants. 'The child could be learning culturally determined patterns that are viewed as appropriate for each sex. Within the limit of his (sic) anatomy, a speaker could change the formant pattern by pronouncing vowels with phonetic variations, or by changing the configuration of the lips' (Sachs et al. 1973:80). So even at an age when their articulatory mechanisms are identical, girls and boys are learning to speak appropriately, that is, to produce higher or lower formants respectively.

Fichtelius et al. showed that both adult and child judges could still guess the sex of a child speaker even when the tapes had been submitted to a process which affects the sound so that individual words and syllables are no longer discernible but rhythmic patterns and intonation are still apparent. Older children were more easily identified than younger ones, since as girls and boys get older, their speech becomes *prosodically* differentiated. Boys begin to employ a more rapid tempo, while girls use a greater variety of intonation patterns.

Children's acquisition of *intonation* has also been investigated by Local (1982) as part of the Tyneside Linguistic Survey. The children were aged between $5\frac{1}{4}$ and 6 by the end of the study. Taped extracts of their speech were abstracted from a larger corpus collected over a period of about a year. Adults on Tyneside use a system of nuclear tone which differs markedly in its frequency distribution from the system used by adult speakers of Standard English. Figure 7.2 (over the page) pictures these differences and shows the gross percentage distribution of each tone in two samples (one of Tyneside speakers, and the other of speakers of Standard English). Note especially the difference in the relative frequency of falls ($\searrow$), rise-falls ($\nearrow\searrow$), and levels ($-$) between the Tyneside and Standard speakers. These differences reflect dialectal differences which enable us to say of a speaker

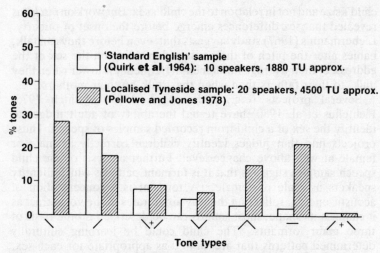

Figure 7.2: Gross percentage distribution of tones for two samples – Tyneside speakers and Standard English speakers (Local 1982:89)

using Tyneside intonation patterns 's/he comes from Tyneside'.

Local shows how the children's tone system altered over the period studied. Most importantly, there was a shift in the relative frequency of falls, rises, and level tones in the children's speech. Further, there was a *decrease* in the frequency of nuclear falls, and an *increase* in the frequency of nuclear levels in the children's speech throughout the period studied. In other words, during the year all the children shifted their speech in the direction of adult Tyneside English. However, the relative frequency of these tones was not the same for all children, and Local identified three different patterns:

Pattern 1: More falls than rises and more levels than rises (Paul, Peter, James, Colin, Robert, Allan)

Pattern 2: More falls than rises and more rises than levels (Keith, Derek, Cath, Eunice, Kate, Judith)

Pattern 3: More rises than falls and more rises than levels (Claire, Angela, Sheila, Janice, Elaine, Anne)

These patterns reveal that the children's speech varies on the basis of sex of speaker. Pattern 3 (more rises than falls or levels) is typical of girls' speech; pattern 1 (falls and levels more frequent than rises) is typical of boys' speech; while pattern 2 is ambiguous, being realised by both girls and boys. Patterns 3 and 1 are also found in adult speech on Tyneside, with adult females using more rises than falls or levels and adult males using more falls and levels than rises. Thus Local's analysis reveals children acquiring not just

Tyneside intonation, but Tyneside intonation appropriate to their sex.

Work on *phonological variation* in children's speech also confirms that sex differentiation is present from an early age. In the course of a study of child-rearing in a semi-rural New England village, Fischer (1964) was struck by differences between the pronunciation of girls and boys. Using his tapes of interviews with the twenty-four children in the sample, he carried out a quantitative analysis of the variable (ing). In this community, (ing) has two variants: the standard variant [ɪŋ] and the non-standard variant [ɪn]. The twenty-four children in the sample consisted of two equal age groups (3–6 year olds, and 7–10 year olds), each group containing equal numbers of girls and boys. Fischer's analysis of his data revealed that the girls used the standard variant [ɪŋ] more frequently, while the boys preferred the non-standard variant [ɪn] (see Table 7.1).

Table 7.1 Sex differences in the use of (ing) (based on Fischer 1964:484)

	More [ɪŋ]	More [ɪn]
Girls	10	2
Boys	5	7

These differences are statistically significant. It seems likely that the children have learned that in their speech community [ɪŋ] is a marker of female speech and [ɪn] is a marker of male speech.

We have already discussed Romaine's (1978) study of primary school children in Edinburgh (see 4.3.4), where Romaine found that sex of speaker was the single most important factor correlating with use of the phonological variable (r). In a survey of sex differences in the language of children and adolescents, Romaine (1984) compares her results for ten year olds in Edinburgh with Macaulay's results for ten year olds in Glasgow (Macaulay's work on *adult* sex differences in Glasgow was discussed in 4.3.2). Although the scoring procedures used in the two studies were slightly different, the results are very similar. Both Romaine and Macaulay investigated the variables (gs) (the glottal stop), (i), (au) and (a), which occur in words like *butter*, *hit*, *house*, and *bag*. For all these variables, there is clear sex differentiation in both Edinburgh and Glasgow (though for (a) in Glasgow the differences in girls' and boys' scores is not large enough to be significant). In other words, girls obtained lower scores than boys for all these variables; their lower scores reflect less frequent use of non-standard variants.[1] The pattern of sex differentiation found

127

among children in Edinburgh and Glasgow is the same as that found in the adult population: the girls consistently prefer forms which are closer to standard pronunciation, while the boys prefer forms which are more non-standard.

It's even possible that these findings greatly underestimate the variation in children's speech. The results discussed here are for 10 year olds; as children get older and move through primary school, their use of non-standard forms appears to diminish, so 10 year olds have lower scores on average than 6 year olds. If we look at the variable (au) in Edinburgh, as used by three different age groups, we can see how the scores get lower, apparently reflecting diminished use of the stigmatised non-standard variant [u:] (as in *hoos*) and increased use of the standard variant [au] (as in *house*).

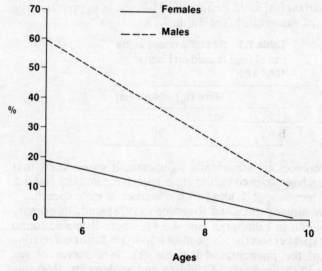

Figure 7.3: Percentage of non-standard [u:] in the usage of girls and boys in three age groups in Edinburgh (Romaine 1984:101)

At the age of 6, the difference between boys' and girls' use of (au) is very marked – boys are shown to choose the non-standard variant [u:] more than 50 per cent of the time (that is, they tend to say *hoos* rather than *house*). Girls at 6, on the other hand, use the non-standard variant less than 20 per cent of the time. As the children get older, both girls and boys are recorded as using fewer stigmatised forms, and the difference between girls' and boys' usage gets smaller.

Romaine suggests that what these figures might actually show is children's growing ability to code-switch, that is, to use different forms in different contexts. She observes that while use of the stigmatised variant certainly decreases in the interview situation as children get older, it is still much in evidence when children are talking among themselves in the playground. So these children can be seen to be acquiring competence in style-shifting (they are learning which styles are appropriate in which contexts), as well as acquiring competence in sex-appropriate linguistic behaviour.

7.3.2 Differences in communicative competence

So far we have looked at work which shows children acquiring the formal features of language. Now we shall examine children's acquisition of sex-differentiated communicative competence. We shall look at work on verbosity, interruptions, politeness, topic, and the so-called 'women's style'.

As far as *verbosity* is concerned, Smith and Connolly (1972) conclude that girls are both more talkative and more fluent. They talk more, both to their mothers and to other children, before the age of four, but after that such quantitative differences disappear. These results could be the result of different expectations on the part of parents. Our culture expects girls and women to talk more and early research in this area, with crude measures and small samples, seemed to confirm the talkativeness of pre-school girls. However, as we saw in Chapter 6 (6.2.2), work on adult language indicates that women talk *less* than men in mixed company. Haas (1978) analysed the amount of speech produced by girls and boys aged 4, 8 and 12 in mixed-sex pairs: she found that boys used longer utterances than girls. This suggests that in mixed groups girls do not talk more than boys – in fact, their behaviour anticipates adult patterns. Perhaps the fluency and loquacity of little girls in test situations is partly the result of the socialisation of little girls into pleasing others – in this case, the girls are pleasing the interviewer.

Research on *interruptions* and *simultaneous speech* has found no significant differences between girls and boys. Parents, however, apparently do differ significantly on both these measures. Greif (1980) studied sixteen middle-class children, aged between 2 and 5, in conversation with (1) their mothers and (2) their fathers. Her results show that fathers interrupted more than mothers (though this difference was not quite large enough to be statistically significant), and that both parents interrupted girls more than boys. In terms of simultaneous speech (that is, both speakers starting to speak at the same time), parents were significantly more likely to continue talking than were children, father-and-child pairs were more likely to engage in simultaneous speech than mother-and-child pairs, and finally both fathers and mothers were more likely to engage in simultaneous speech with daughters than with sons.

As we have seen (6.2.1), the use of interruptions and simultaneous speech can be interpreted as a way of controlling conversation. It seems that fathers try to control conversation more than mothers (which fits the research results for adult conversations), and both parents try to control conversation more with daughters than with sons. The implicit message to girls is that they are more interruptible and that their right to speak is less than that of boys.

Politeness is another dimension of communicative competence where we find sex differences (see 6.3). Research on child language has concentrated on the way parents teach polite language, for example, formulae like greetings and *thank you*. Gleason (1980) studied parents and children in both natural and laboratory settings. She was interested in finding out how much *explicit* teaching of such formulae goes on. She found parents very consistent in prompting their children to respond with socially appropriate items, particularly *thank you*. Parents treated girls and boys similarly, but provided different models: the mothers used far more polite speech than the fathers. Thus, while girls and boys are both urged to use polite forms, the children observe that it is predominantly adult females who use them themselves. The one significant difference observed of the children was that the boys were more likely than the girls to greet the researcher spontaneously (41 per cent: 18 per cent). This may also result from the children's observation of adults: adult male speakers tend to take the initiative in conversation.

Politeness is a relevant dimension for the speech act of requesting. A request may vary from the blunt imperative. *Give me a pound* to the more polite (because sensitive to the face needs of the addressee – see 6.3) *Would you lend me a pound?*. Walters (1981) observed the requests of thirty-two bilingual children in four different contexts. He found no significant differences in terms of the sex of the speaker, but the sex of the addressee was significantly correlated with the politeness of the request. The children in the study were more polite when the addressee was female, and less polite when the addressee was male.

The primary function of the modal expression *I think* is to express subjective uncertainty or deference. By using *I think* to express deference, by hedging the force of an assertion and thus taking account of the face needs of the addressee, speakers mark their speech as more polite. Consider the following example: '*It's a beech tree I think*' (Mother disagreeing with child). In such an example, the phrase *I think* mitigates the force of a negatively affective utterance. In his work on children's acquisition of modal expressions, Perkins (1983) found that *I think* was used by significantly more girls (61.3 per cent) than boys (38.7 per cent). He suggests that this finding lends support to the idea that in acquiring communicative competence, girls are learning to be unassertive.

The larger question of a separate *female style* is addressed in the two studies of child language to be described below, those of Haas (1978) and Edelsky (1976). Haas (1978) analysed the speech of 4-, 8- and 12-year old children in same-sex and mixed-sex pairs. In same-sex pairs, the main difference between girls and boys was that boys talked significantly more about sports and location, while girls talked significantly more about school, identity, wishes and needs. Haas's comparison of mixed-sex pairs also found a difference related to topic – the subject of sport was significantly associated with boy speakers. Boys also used more sound effects (e.g. *brrmm brrmm goes the car*) and more direct requests. The girls laughed more and used more compliant forms (e.g. *okay that's a good idea*). The girl's use of laughter was far more prominent in their interaction with boys than in same-sex interaction – they laughed only half as much when talking to each other. Haas comments that boys seemed to be the initiators of humour, and laughter was the girls' response to this. Laughter may also be seen as appropriately deferential behaviour by the girls, and therefore occurs more with the boys. Both girls and boys adapted their linguistic behaviour when in mixed pairs, but girls accommodated to boys more than vice versa.

Children are acquiring not only sex-appropriate behaviour, but also a knowledge of the folklinguistic beliefs of our society. At what age do children learn that in our culture swearing, for example, is considered 'masculine'? Edelsky (1976) tested this by selecting twelve language variables conventionally associated with 'women's language' or with 'men's language' and presenting them, embedded in utterances, to adult and child judges. The judges were asked to rate each sentence as probably made by a woman, probably made by a man, or no preference. Her child judges (aged 7, 9 and 12 years) demonstrated a growing ability to recognise certain linguistic forms as appropriate to speakers of a particular sex. At 7 years, only two variables get a consistent response: *adorable* is judged to be female, and *Damn it!* is judged to be male. At 9 years, this has increased to eight variables: *adorable, oh dear, my goodness, won't you please* are judged to be female, *and damn it!, damn* + adjective, *I'll be damned* are judged to be male (tag questions get a neutral response). At 12 years, the child judges agree on assigning every one of the twelve variables to one sex or the other: tag questions, *so, very, just* are added to the female list, and commands to the male list.

We can see that children are gradually acquiring a knowledge of adult norms, and internalising the folklinguistic beliefs of our society (the fact that some of these beliefs are false – see

131

discussion, 6.2 – is irrelevant). Edelsky gives a more delicate analysis of her findings to show that there are two clear patterns of acquisition. Variables in her first group – *adorable, oh dear, my goodness, so, just*, tag questions – show a steady increase with age in the number of people able to interpret them as being appropriate to a particular sex. Variables in the second group – *I'll be damned, damn* + adjective, *damnit, won't you please, very*, command as male – show a different pattern: there is an increase in 'correct' answers peaking at twelve years old and decreasing in adulthood. It seems that the variables in this second group are features of language which are explicitly commented on through proverbs or admonishments. Expressions such as 'Little girls don't say that' mean that children are *taught* the sex-appropriateness of some linguistic items. As happens with other features of child language, when a rule is learned it is frequently over-generalised. Just as children add *-ed* to all verbs to form the past tense, once they've grasped this rule, producing forms like *goed, eated, signed*, (even though they earlier used forms like *went, ate, sang* – and of course subsequently do so again), so it seems they over-generalise the rule for sex-appropriate language and treat such differences as *sex-exclusive* rather than *sex-preferential*. As a result, they have to modify their rules later to conform to adult norms.

It seems that adult interaction with girls and boys may be significantly affected by *context*. In a long-term study of children in Bristol, Wells (1979) examined all conversations occurring when the children were 3¼ years old, and categorised them according to who initiated them (the child or the adult) and according to the context (mealtime, watching television, playing with another child, etc.). 30 per cent of conversation sequences were initiated by an adult (usually the mother), and an analysis of these revealed significant differences in the context in which adults addressed girls or boys. Table 7.2 gives the figures.

Table 7.2 Proportions of conversations initiated by adults with girls and boys in different contexts (based on Wells 1979:391)

	% Girls	% Boys
Helping/non-play activity	56.8	28.8
Talking and reading	19.0	22.5
Playing with adult	5.2	18.1
Dressing, meals, toileting	12.1	14.4
Playing alone	3.4	8.1
Watching TV	0.9	5.4
Playing with another child	2.6	2.7
TOTAL:	100	100

This table shows that over half the sequences initiated with girls were in helping or non-play contexts – a ratio of 2:1 compared with the boys. Sequences initiated with boys, on the other hand, were overwhelmingly in the context of play. 'This suggests that adults emphasize more useful and domestic activities in their interaction with girls, whilst the emphasis with boys is towards a more free-ranging, exploratory manipulation of the physical environment' (Wells 1979:392).

7.4 CONCLUSION

As we have seen, various studies show differences in male and female children in a wide range of linguistic forms. What emerges is a picture of girls acquiring linguistic skills at a faster rate than boys (though this superiority is not as marked as was claimed in the past), and acquiring patterns which differentiate them from boys. In the past, researchers believed that such differences arose from innate biological differences, but now differences in linguistic usage are explained by differences in the linguistic environment of girls and boys. Work on the development of differential communicative competence illustrates particularly clearly the crucial role played by environmental factors.

Language is an important part of the socialisation process, and children are socialised into culturally approved sex roles largely through language. Learning to be male or female in our society means among other things learning to use sex-appropriate language. This survey of work on children's acquisition of language suggests that socialisation is achieved in four ways:

1. through explicit comment on certain aspects of linguistic behaviour (e.g. swearing, taboo language, verbosity, politeness);

2. through adults providing different linguistic models for children to identify with (see also Chapters 4, 5 and 6);

3. through adults talking to children differently depending on the sex of the child (e.g. adults are more likely to interrupt girls, and lisp more when talking to little girls);

4. through adults having different preconceptions of male and female children (e.g. adults expect female infants to be more verbally able than male infants).

It is often suggested that child language may be the locus of linguistic change: that is, a comparison of the variety of language acquired by children with the variety used by adults of the same ethnic group, social class, etc. will reveal linguistic change in progress. We shall turn now from our survey of child language and the acquisition of sex-preferential differences to an examination of the role these sex differences play in the process of linguistic change.

NOTE

1 Both Romaine and Macaulay adopted scoring procedures which represent RP with a score of 0.

Chapter Eight

The role of sex differences in linguistic change

8.1   INTRODUCTION

One of the linguistic consequences of sex differentiation in language seems to be linguistic change. Certainly, differences in women's and men's language are regularly associated with changes in language.

Yet it is only recently that sociolinguistic factors have been taken into consideration by linguists studying language change. Linguists have traditionally preferred to treat language as a closed system which could be studied without reference to 'external' factors. Linguistic study, in other words, has until recently been a-social. The neogrammarians – nineteenth-century comparative philologists – argued that linguistic change was caused by the twin mechanisms of sound change and analogy: sound change altered the system, and analogy made the system regular again. The functionalists on the other hand – linguists who treated the notion of function as central – argued that change occurs because of the opposing demands of the need to communicate and the desire to make as little effort as possible.

The most striking thing about this debate is the way it *reifies* language, that is, treats language as a *thing*, existing in its own right. Language does not, however, exist apart from language users; speech does not exist independently of speakers. So we need to make a distinction between linguistic change, which is change in the language system, and speaker innovation, which describes the role played by speakers in initiating linguistic change (for an illuminating discussion of this distinction, see Milroy and Milroy 1985). The study of linguistic change has a long history, but our understanding of the role played by individual speakers is still in its infancy.

Linguistic change occurs in the context of linguistic heterogeneity. Linguistic variation exists in all known societies: it distinguishes the speech of different social groups (**social variation**), and it distinguishes the speech of a given individual in different contexts (**stylistic variation**). Linguistic change can be said to have taken place when a new linguistic form, used by some sub-group within a speech community, is adopted by other members of that community and accepted as the norm. Our understanding of the interaction of groups within society is still poor, but we are beginning to see that the linguistic variation which characterises the differentiation of social groups is crucially associated with the rise and fall of linguistic forms.

In this book, we have focused on the linguistic variation associated with speaker's sex. Sociolinguistic research is beginning to improve our understanding of linguistic change, and it now seems that sex differentiation in speech plays an important role in the mechanism of linguistic change. More accurately, the sex of the speaker plays a significant part in innovation – sometimes women and sometimes men are said to be the group which typically initiates change. This debate parallels that described earlier in dialectology (3.5.1) on whether women or men are more conservative linguistically. We shall return to this issue later. In this chapter we shall look at work demonstrating (or claiming to demonstrate) a link between sex differences in language and linguistic change. We shall look first at earlier (dialectological) work, and then, in greater detail, at some recent sociolinguistic studies. In this latter section we shall refer back to studies already discussed in Chapter 4 and 5.

8.2 DIALECTOLOGICAL EVIDENCE

Dialectologists discussed linguistic change in the communities they studied, sometimes in terms of changing patterns of bilingualism, sometimes in terms of changes in vocabulary or pronunciation within one language system. Since they were often trying to make a record of rural dialects before they died out, they were very aware that linguistic change was taking place, and their comments on the social background of such changes are of great interest.

Auguste Brun, a specialist in the language known as Provençal, discusses the relative roles of Provençal and French in one particular community (Brun 1946). He observes that older people (over 50) speak mainly Provençal, as do younger men, but *women* under 45 speak mainly French. He claims that younger women do not speak Provençal at all among themselves ('je n'ai jamais entendu une phrase de provençal dans une groupe de jeunes filles ou de jeunes femmes'), nor do they speak Provençal to their children, but only occasionally to the old people, As a result, children of both sexes speak French: they don't speak Provençal to each other or to adults (Brun, as quoted in Pop 1950:281). If Brun's observations are accurate, we see that in three generations this community has switched from being bilingual but mainly Provençal-speaking to being bilingual but mainly French-speaking, with the use of Provençal diminishing rapidly. Women are portrayed as having a crucial role, since it is they and not the men who adopt French as their main language, and they who use it when bringing up the next generation. At all events, the difference between male and female usage is clearly a crucial factor in the linguistic change described here.

Pée's (1946) account of changing linguistic usage in Flanders is interesting because he is able to give the background to the change described. The older generation, according to Pée, speak patois (varieties of Flemish); Pée found the women particularly good as informants because of their lack of mobility – they hardly ever left their village and so had little contact with other linguistic varieties. But the First World War resulted in an improved standard of living for many peasants, some of whom sent their daughters to French boarding schools. These girls became 'francisées' (Frenchified/Francophile) and insisted on speaking French instead of Flemish when they returned home. Only those who then worked on the land reverted to Flemish. Pée reports that the girls back from boarding school asked for the sermon at least to be in French at Mass on a Sunday. Clearly the girls in this community were initiating change, and the balance between Flemish and French was changing as a result of their influence.

Gilliéron studied a monolingual French community, and he comments on changes taking place in vocabulary there. He quotes the Torgon peasant who told him: 'In the past the room where we are was called *le pailé*, now we call it *la tsābra*, and my wife, who wants to be more refined than us, calls it *Kabiné*'[1]. This remark by one of Gilliéron's informants reveals three stages in the linguistic evolution of a lexical item: an old form – *pailé*, a current form – *tsābra*; and a new advanced form – *kabiné*. It is women again who are innovating, using the most advanced form (for status reasons, according to the peasant).

Gauchat's (1905) study of the dialect of Charmey, a remote village in Switzerland, shows a great sensitivity to the social context in which linguistic evolution takes place. He observed that the old inhabitants of the village used forms which were phonetically older than those beginning to be used by the young people. He noted that among people of the same age, the women's pronunciation was more advanced. In other words, there were sex differences as well as age differences in the language of the

137

community (he had chosen Charmey to try to avoid linguistic variation!). He argues that changes have occurred in French because of women's innovativeness ('les femmes accueillaient . . . avec empressement toute nouveauté linguistique') and that these changes are disseminated by women in their role as mothers: 'Once the woman has accepted the innovation, it is from *her* language that this will pass into the language of the young, because children tend to follow their mother's example'[2]. As this extract shows, Gauchat was one of those dialectologists who believed that women were an innovatory rather than a conservative force. It is clearly a logical extension of this position to argue that women, in their role as primary caretakers of children, initiate linguistic change. We will pursue this argument in 8.4.

As these four examples from dialectology show, women are frequently portrayed as playing a crucial role in initiating and furthering linguistic change. However, as the following sociolinguistic examples will demonstrate, this is an over-simplistic picture, as some innovations are clearly associated with male rather than with female speakers.

8.3 SOCIOLINGUISTIC STUDIES SHOWING CHANGE IN PROGRESS

Linguists used to think that linguistic change was something which could not be observed: 'such observation . . . is inconceivable' (Bloomfield 1933:347). This misconception was partly the result of de Saussure's division of linguistic study into **synchronic** and **diachronic**: synchronic study took language at one point in time, while diachronic study took language *through* time, comparing language at different points in time to see how it changed. The study of change, then, was firmly linked with **diachronic** linguistics. It is only with the advent of sociolinguistics, specifically with the work of William Labov, that linguists have demonstrated that linguistic change is amenable to analysis. Quantitative studies, analysing synchronic variation in language, have the capacity to reveal change in progress.

The best-known diagram of change in progress is Labov's diagram for post-vocalic (r) in New York City which is reproduced in Figure 8.1 opposite. We have already discussed this briefly in 4.2.2. Note again the hypercorrect pattern of the lower middle class, with very low scores for (r) usage in Casual Speech, rising to extremely high scores (higher than the upper middle class) in the two most formal styles. The crossover pattern this produces is said by Labov to be typical of a variable undergoing change. 'The hypercorrect behaviour of the lower middle class is

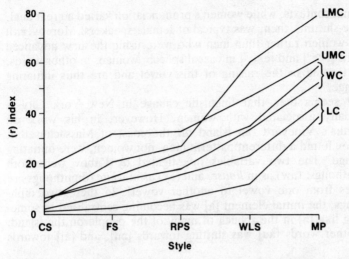

Figure 8.1: Social stratification of a linguistic variable undergoing change – post-vocalic (r) in New York City (Labov 1972a:114)

seen as a synchronic indicator of linguistic change in progress' (Labov, 1972a:115).

In his earlier work, Labov reflected the prevailing view that women were innovators. He included a section on 'The Role of Women' in his chapter on 'The Social Setting of Linguistic Change' (Labov 1972a:301–4), where he claimed that women played an important part in linguistic change. However, more recently he has modified his views, and now argues that change is precipitated by linguistic differences between the sexes rather than being associated with one particular sex. As we shall see, this latter view accords far better with his own findings.

We shall therefore look first at the work of Labov himself in this field, both his analysis of (a) in New York City and his study of centralised diphthongs on Martha's Vineyard. We shall then re-examine the work of Romaine in Edinburgh, Trudgill in Norwich, and Milroy in Belfast (as discussed in Chapters 4 and 5), paying particular attention this time to the relationship between sex differences in language and linguistic change.

8.3.1 New York City and Martha's Vineyard

Many of the variables studied by Labov in New York City were in the process of change, and he was able to show significant sex differences in their usage. With the variable (a)[3] (the short vowel found in words like *bag, ham, cab*), for example, Labov found that men's pronunciation varied very little between formal and less formal contexts, while women's pronunciation varied a great deal. Style-shifting, then, was typical of female speakers. Moreover, it was women rather than men who were using the new advanced forms [i<:ᵊ] and [e<:ᵊ] in casual speech; women, in other words, are leading in the raising of this vowel and are thus initiating change.

It seems then that linguistic change in New York City is crucially associated with women, However, in his work on Martha's Vineyard (an island off the coast of Massachusetts), Labov found a different pattern: men, not women, were initiating change. The two variables investigated by Labov were both diphthongs: (aw) as in *house*, and (ay) as in *white* (diphthongs are glides from one vowel to another vowel). In these two diphthongs, the initial element [a] was becoming centralised to something like [ə] in the speech of many of the people on the island. In other words [au] was shifting towards [əu], and [ai] towards [əi].

Labov conducted interviews with 69 informants; he included only members of the permanent population and excluded the summer visitors. He realised that there was no conscious awareness among the islanders that these sounds were fluctuating, since he found no *stylistic* variation – individuals' pronunciation of the diphthongs was consistent in different styles of speech. He established that the centralised variants were used mostly by *men* (specifically fishermen) aged between 31 and 45 from an area at the western end of the island called Chilmark. It seems that the centralised diphthongs were used by the Chilmark fishermen as a sign of solidarity; use of these variants symbolised their identification with the island and its values, and their rejection of the summer visitors.

These centralised diphthongs are actually very old. They were conservative features of the fishermen's speech which are now spreading to the speech of other islanders. In other words, an older form, which was in the process of dying out, has now become a significant feature of the island phonology; a linguistic change has reversed direction.

What quantitative studies such as this reveal in **change in apparent time**, that is, fluctuating usage at one particular point in time. By consulting the Linguistic Atlas of New England and other earlier surveys of pronunciation in this region. Labov was able to confirm that this is actually a **change in real time** (diachronic change). As we shall see, this practice of testing findings against earlier historical records is common in sociolinguistic work charting change in progress.

Linguistic change on Martha's Vineyard, then, has been initiated by a group of *male* speakers, the Chilmark fishermen.

Their speech, with its centralised diphthongs, was once seen as old-fashioned, but at some stage, as local feeling grew stronger in the face of the invading 'outsider' (the summer visitors), this type of speech become symbolic of belonging to the island, of being an 'insider'. Note that it is still primarily male speakers who use these centralised diphthongs. Thus the change begins with, and is imitated by, men.

Labov's New York survey shows *women* in the vanguard of linguistic change, while the study of Martha's Vineyard reveals a linguistic change in progress which originated with *male* speakers. As we shall see in the following sections, these two contrasting patterns are found in other studies of linguistic change in progress.

8.3.2 Edinburgh

We have already described the results of Romaine's investigation of post-vocalic (r) in Edinburgh (4.3.4). Irregularities in the pattern of age, style and sex differentiation for this variable led her to believe that linguistic change was taking place. Most importantly, she confirmed that r-lessness, previously unrecorded, was now a feature of Edinburgh speech.

As we saw in 4.3.4, sex of speaker was the single most important factor correlating with use of post-vocalic (r). The diagram (Figure 8.2) showing the results for male and female speech is reproduced to show again the contrast between male and female scores for the three variants [ɾ], [ɹ] and Ø. Male speakers consistently use more of the [ɾ] variant than female

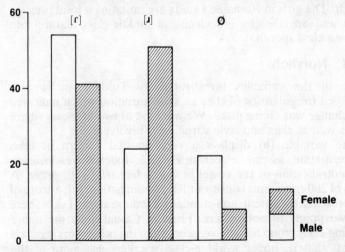

Figure 8.2: Sex differences in the use of the variable (r) in Edinburgh based on Romaine 1978:150)

speakers, and are also more likely to use Ø. Girls on the other hand consistently prefer the frictionless continuant [ɹ] and avoid r-less pronunciation. Note the crossover pattern this variation produces, which signals linguistic change in progress. The pattern of style differentiation differs from that found for other variables studied by Romaine in Edinburgh. The use of both [ɹ] and Ø increased in Reading Passage Style (more formal style). This suggests that, although the fluctuation of (r) between styles was not great, there is some low-level awareness of (r) in the community, and that both [ɹ] and Ø have prestige.

Romaine investigated accounts of (r) in Scottish speech in the past. Both Williams (1912) and Grant (1914) provide detailed descriptions of (r) pronunciation at the turn of the century. They record that (r) was normally pronounced as a trilled consonant [r], sometimes reduced to a single tap [ɾ]. The frictionless continuant [ɹ] is also recorded, but the trilled [r] is said to be the most common as well as the socially preferred form. Romaine's findings establish that pronunciation of word-final (r) is still fluctuating, and that there has been a change in real time with the emergence of r-less pronunciation.

Romaine argues that change is being brought about in two ways. Firstly, the loss of post-vocalic (r) – that is, use of Ø – is being initiated by younger working-class speakers from one particular area of the city. These speakers are *male*. The other innovation is the use of [ɹ], the frictionless continuant, by working-class *female* speakers. The variant [ɹ] has been associated for many years with middle-class speech in Scotland, particularly female speech. The girls in Romaine's study are imitating a local prestige norm and are thereby introducing a middle-class feature into working-class speech.

8.3.3 Norwich

Some of the variables investigated by Trudgill in Norwich displayed irregularities of class or style variation which indicated that change was taking place. We will look at two of these, where sex as well as class and style variation is involved.

The variable (e) displays a very unusual pattern of class differentiation, as can be seen in Fig. 8.3. Index scores measure the centralisation of the vowel in words like *tell*, *well*, *better*. A score of 200 represents consistent RP pronunciation: [ɛ]; a score of 0 represents consistent non-standard pronunciation: [ʌ].[4] There are two points to notice here. First, in Casual Style the *upper* working-class group has a *lower* score than the other working-class groups, that is, upper working-class speakers use more of the non-standard centralised variant. Second, in *all* styles the upper and middle working-class groups use more of the non-standard

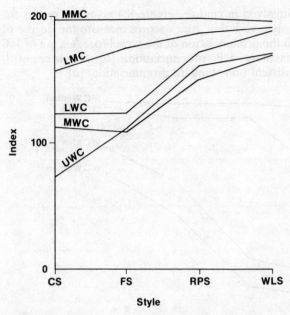

Figure 8.3: Social stratification of (e) in Norwich (based on Trudgill 1974a:105)

variant than the lower working class. So while the stratification of the middle class as a whole and the working class as a whole is as expected, the pattern of groups *within* the working class is upside down, with the upper working-class using the highest proportion of non-standard variants.

Trudgill observes that centralisation of (e) is increasing in Norwich, and this change is being innovated by the upper working-class. He notes that the use of centralised variants is associated not only with upper working-class speakers but also with *male* speakers under thirty. Younger speakers have much lower scores than older speakers, and male speakers have lower scores than female speakers. In the youngest age group studied by Trudgill (10–19), male and female speakers differed significantly: the average score for the young male speakers was 0 indicating consistent use of the centralised vowel.

We can summarise these findings by saying that the variable (e) in Norwich is undergoing change, this change is manifest in the irregular pattern of class stratification, and the change is being innovated by young *male* upper working-class speakers in particular.

The variable (o), the vowel occurring in words like *top*, *fog*,

143

lorry, is also involved in change. Figure 8.4 gives the results for class, sex and style variation: index scores measure the degree of lip-rounding in the pronunciation of the vowel (o). A score of 100 represents consistent RP pronunciation: [ɒ]; a score of 0 represents consistent non-standard pronunciation: [ɑ].[4]

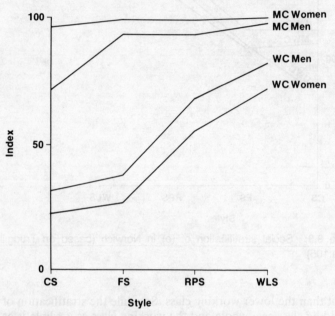

Figure 8.4: Stratification of (o) in Norwich by social class and sex (based on Trudgill 1972:189)

This diagram reveals a striking irregularity in the stratification of speakers. Middle-class women use a virtually consistent RP pronunciation of (o); they score higher than middle-class men in all styles. Working-class women, on the other hand, consistently score *lower* than working-class men; in all styles the diagram shows that working-class women used a higher proportion of the non-standard variant [a]. What is the explanation for this unusual pattern? (compare it with the expected pattern shown in Fig. 4.5, p. 63). It seems that working-class *men* are innovating with the pronunciation [ɒ], imitating local Suffolk working-class speech (Norfolk speech has traditionally used the unrounded vowel [ɑ]). This change happens to coincide with the standard (RP) form, which is used predominantly by middle-class *women*. Thus, middle-class women are conforming to the prestige norm, while working-class women are conforming to an older vernacular norm; working-class men, however, are innovating with a new vernacular norm. The coincidence of this Suffolk vernacular form with the prestige form means that working-class men's scores are closer to those of the middle-class. With this variable, it is the irregularity in the pattern of sex differentiation which signals change in progress.

8.3.4 Belfast

Several of the variables studied by the Milroys in Belfast are in the process of change. We shall look at two of them – (ε) and (a) – since in both cases linguistic change is associated with sex-differentiated usage.

The variable (ε) occurs in words like *step*, *peck*, *bet*, and variants range from [a] to [ɛ]. The variable is undergoing raising, and the new prestigious raised variants of (ε) are being introduced by women, particularly younger women. Figure 8.5 shows the distribution of (ε) in 'short' phonetic environments, that is, where the vowel is followed by a voiceless stop: [p, t, k].

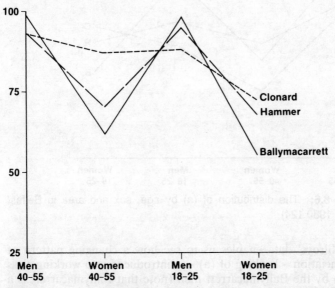

Figure 8.5: The distribution of (ε) by age, sex and area in Belfast (Milroy and Milroy 1978:30)

Note the clear sex-differentiation involved in the use of this variable; this is particularly marked in Ballymacarrett. For many male speakers, the low short variant [a] or [æ] is categorical before voiceless stops. Both older and younger men in Ballymacarrett score 100, that is, use the low short variant consistently. The younger women in all three communities have much lower scores

145

than the men, reflecting their preference for raised variants. Comparison with historical records leads the Milroys to conclude that the raising of (ε) is a change in real time. Change is being initiated by younger female speakers who are introducing a new high-status variant into inner-city Belfast.

The variable (a) is also undergoing change, but here the pattern is different. Backing of (a) is in progress, and backed variants are typical of Ballymacarrett speakers and typical of *male* speakers. In other words, men are more likely than women to pronounce *man* [mɔ.ən]. Figure 8.6 shows the distribution of (a) in the three communities.

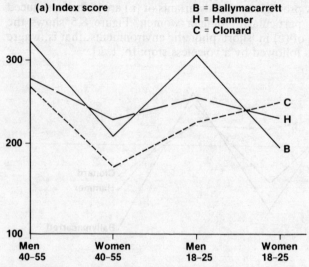

Figure 8.6: The distribution of (a) by age, sex and area in Belfast (Milroy 1980:124)

The Milroys' data enables us to see how a changing pattern of pronunciation – backing of (a) – is introduced into working-class speech by the Ballymacarrett men (note that Ballymacarrett is a stable and prestigious community). This new vernacular variant is then adopted by another sub-group, the Clonard young women. As Fig. 8.6 shows, young women in the Clonard score higher than the young men of their community and also higher than the Ballymacarrett young women. This produces the crossover pattern typical of a linguistic change in progress. The young Clonard women, then, are introducing into their own community a variant of (a) borrowed from a higher ranking community. (In Belfast, Protestant ranks higher than Catholic.) Backing of (a) is spreading from East to West Belfast, from a high ranking to a low ranking working-class community.

By consulting early records of Belfast pronunciation (Patterson 1860), the Milroys have established that (a) was not normally backed in 1860. Thus we have evidence, in both apparent and real time, that a linguistic change is taking place, and again we find that the variable in question is involved in sex differentiation. It seems that backing of (a) has the status of a vernacular norm and is typical of speakers belonging to close-knit working-class groups; the young Clonard women belong, like the Ballymacarret men, to dense, multiplex networks. While unemployment in the Hammer has led to a breakdown of networks and a corresponding blurring of sex differences, male unemployment in the Clonard has led to the younger women seeking work, finding work together, and developing a pattern of social interaction similar to the traditional pattern for working-class *men*. This change in social pattern has resulted in a changing *linguistic* pattern for the Clonard community, with the young women acting as innovators. As we can see, changes in network structure can be an important social mechanism of linguistic change.

We have described two variables in the process of change in inner-city Belfast. Prestigious raised variants of (ε) are being introduced into Belfast speech by younger *women*, while backing of (a) has been introduced by Ballymacarrett *men* and this new vernacular norm is now being adopted by the young Clonard women.

8.4 SEX DIFFERENTIATION AND LINGUISTIC CHANGE

The dialectological evidence given in 8.2 shows women as innovators; the sociolinguistic evidence given in 8.3 shows both women and men initiating linguistic change. In order to make sense of these two patterns, one involving women as innovators, the other involving men as innovators, we need to distinguish between **conscious** and **unconscious** change, or 'change from above' and 'change from below' as Labov calls them (Labov 1972a). There are some linguistic changes which speakers are conscious of and which are actively encouraged: these tend to be associated with the middle class. There are other changes which go on *below* the level of public consciousness: these tend to be associated with the working class. Women seem to initiate changes above the level of social awareness: such changes tend to be in the direction of the prestige norms. Men, on the other hand, seem to initiate changes below the level of social awareness: such changes tend to be *away from* the accepted norms.

The shift to centralised diphthongs on Martha's Vineyard is a good example of change taking place *below* the level of social awareness. According to Labov, the native Vineyarders are not aware of this feature in their language. As a result, he found no style shifting associated with the diphthongs; speakers have no control over this feature in their speech and their pronunciation is therefore the same whatever the context. As we have seen, it is *men* who are (unconsciously) initiating and furthering this change in the local language.

Labov's work in New York City revealed several variables where change was taking place *above* the level of consciousness. Figure 8.1 – postvocalic (r) – is a very good example of this. Note the steep slope for all groups: (r) is clearly subject to a great deal of style-shifting, with the lower middle-class in particular shifting from low usage of (r) in casual speech to very high usage of (r) in Word List Style. The variable (a) – see 8.3.1 – is another typical example of change taking place from above the level of consciousness. Here it is women who are revealed as being particularly conscious of the variant, as is shown by the extent of their style-shifting.

In Belfast, female speakers are innovating towards a *prestige* norm with raised variants of (ε), while male speakers are responsible for the introduction of a new *vernacular* norm, backing of (a), to the inner city. In both Norwich and Edinburgh, change is taking place in two directions at once, with female speakers innovating towards a prestige norm and male speakers innovating away from the prestige norm. In Norwich, as we have seen, the rural Suffolk vernacular norm which working-class men are taking as their model happens to coincide with the RP norm which female speakers are imitating. This fortuitous coincidence of change from below with change from above means that the shift to the rounded vowel (that is, [ɒ] in place of traditional Norwich [ɑ]) has a good chance of success. In Edinburgh, the two groups are innovating in two different directions, which leads to the complex pattern displayed in Fig. 8.2. It will be interesting to see whether the female [ɪ] variant or the male Ø variant gains more prestige in the future. The girls' variant has high prestige in Scotland, particularly in educational circles. The variant preferred by the boys, however, an innovation not previously recorded for Edinburgh, happens to coincide with English RP: this may affect the outcome of this particular sound change.

Many sociolinguists have argued that linguistic change is associated with women, particularly women of the lower middle class. These linguists also tend to adhere to the belief that it is women in their role as *mothers*, bringing up the next generation, who facilitate language change. The data presented in this chapter reveals a less simple pattern. Some change does indeed seem to be initiated by women. Such change is often in the direction of prestige norms, and patterns of style shifting reveal it to be change of which speakers are conscious. But some linguistic change is initiated by men, often working-class men. This is more often change away from prestige norms, which is taking place below the level of conscious awareness.

As for the notion that women bring about change in their role as mothers, this does not seem tenable in the face of the evidence. Firstly, when men are the innovators, is it in their role as fathers that they disseminate change? Clearly not. Secondly, what we know about speakers and linguistic behaviour shows us that speakers are influenced by their *peers* rather than by their parents; change occurs when speakers imitate the speech of a sub-group with whom they wish to identify.

What is the explanation for the two patterns of change we have described? It seems as though women are more sensitive to status-giving prestige norms (whether the prestige norms are those of Standard English or those of a higher-ranked group, as in the case of the Clonard young women imitating the prestigious Ballymacarret community), while men are more sensitive to vernacular norms, which represent solidarity and values traditionally associated with masculinity. Two factors frequently put forward in the past to 'explain' women's linguistic behaviour were sensitivity and conservatism. (Note that men's language was taken as given and so did not need explaining.) As we have seen, both women and men are linguistically sensitive, but to different models. Women's conservatism is merely the converse of male innovation: when male speakers initiate change, then women speakers can be described as conservative – they conserve older forms. Conversely, when female speakers initiate change, then male speakers can be described as conservative (though conservatism is not often ascribed to men, except in the work of traditional dialectologists). Conservatism and sensitivity are two sides of the same coin, and neither sex has the monopoly of either of them.

The idea that only middle-class women are innovative seems no longer tenable when we observe the working-class Edinburgh girls who are innovating with [ɪ], and the Clonard young women in Belfast who are leading the change to a more backed (a) in their community. This may be because of changing structures in society. Lesley Milroy observes that use of vernacular norms is connected with membership of dense, multiplex social networks. In traditional working-class communities it was men who belonged to such networks, and whose speech was closest to the vernacular. With growing unemployment, and changes in sex roles, it seems that younger women are now using more consistent vernacular speech as they adopt a more 'male' life-style, and accordingly belong to close-knit social networks.

As we have said, linguistic change can only take place in the context of linguistic variation, and linguistic variation is merely a reflection of social variation. Societies vary in all kinds of ways, but male and female roles are distinguished in some way in all known societies. It is not surprising, then, that the linguistic variation arising from socially constructed differences between women and men turns out to have a significant role in facilitating linguistic evolution.

In conclusion, it is not true to say that either women or men are linguistically the innovative sex. As we have seen, some linguistic change is initiated by female speakers and some by male speakers. However, it is true to say that male/female differences in language seem to be intimately involved in the mechanism of linguistic change. This being the case, the study of linguistic change can only benefit from the growing interest in the sociolinguistic analysis of sex differentiation in speech.

Notes

1 'Autrefois la chambre où nous sommes, on la nommait le *pailé*, maintenant nous l'appelons la *tsābra*, et ma femme, qui veut être plus fine que nous, la nomme *kabiné* (Gilliéron 1880:iv, as quoted in Pop 1950:180).

2 'Une fois que la femme a accepté l'innovation, c'est de son langage que celle-ci passera dans le langage de la jeunesse, parce que les enfants suivent plutot l'exemple des femmes' (Gauchat 1905:218, quoted in Pop 1950:194).

3 Labov labels this variable (eh).

4 Trudgill actually scores these variables the other way round, with the highest score representing consistent *non*-standard pronunciation, and 0 representing the prestige form. For consistency in this book (see Chapter 4), all figures showing social stratification have been presented in the same way.

Chapter Nine

The social consequences of linguistic sex differences

9.1 INTRODUCTION

This chapter will examine the social, as opposed to linguistic, consequences of linguistic differentiation based on sex. First, the problem of miscommunication between women and men will be assessed in the light of current knowledge of interaction patterns; second, the question of disadvantage will be raised in the context of the differing linguistic behaviour of girls and boys in the classroom. Work on miscommunication in adult conversation tends to take sex differences in language as a given, and concentrates on the specific aspects of conversational interaction where communication between women and men can break down. Studies of classroom interaction, by contrast, tend to be critical of the social pressures which bring about linguistic sex differences. Many researchers feel that girls are failing to fulfil their potential in school, and that language is one of the contributing factors – they are therefore not content to adopt a different-but-equal stance.

9.2 MISCOMMUNICATION BETWEEN WOMEN AND MEN

As we saw in Chapter 6 (section 6.5), there is considerable evidence that the patterns of interaction typical of all-women groups differ from those typical of all-men groups.[1] I shall summarise this evidence here, before enumerating the sites of potential miscommunication. In all-women groups, women often discuss one topic for half an hour or more; they share a great deal of information about themselves and talk about their feelings and their relationships. Men on the other hand jump from one topic to another, vying to tell anecdotes which centre around themes of superiority and aggression. They rarely talk about themselves, but compete to prove themselves better informed about current affairs, travel, sport, etc. The *management* of conversation also differs significantly between women's and men's groups. Women are careful to respect each other's turns and tend to apologise for talking too much. Members of all-women groups are concerned that everyone should participate and dislike any one person dominating conversation. Men in all-men groups, by contrast, compete for dominance and over time establish a reasonably stable hierarchy, with some men dominating conversation and others talking very little. Individual men frequently address the whole group (33 per cent of the time on average, in Aries's (1976) experimental groups), while individual women rarely do (6.5 per cent of the time on average), preferring an interpersonal style involving one-to-one interaction.[2]

Maltz and Borker (1982) have analysed some of the ways in which these differences could cause miscommunication in mixed conversations. I shall look at seven problem areas, elaborating on them in the light of earlier discussion.

The meaning of questions

Questions seem to have a different meaning for women and men. As we saw in 6.2.2, women use questions more than men – they use them as part of a general strategy for conversational maintenance: questions are speech acts which require a subsequent speech act – an answer – so using questions is a way of ensuring that a conversation continues. It seems that men, by contrast, interpret questions as simple requests for information. We have here a clash between direct and indirect modes: men interpret questions at face value while women see them as facilitating the flow of conversation. This is clearly an area which has the potential for miscommunication.

Links between speaker turns

When a speaker takes a turn in conversation, s/he can begin by explicitly acknowledging the contribution of the previous speaker(s) and can then talk on a topic directly connected with what has gone before. It seems that this is a pattern typically adopted by women. Men on the other hand do not feel they have to make a link with the previous speaker's contribution; on the contrary, men are more likely to ignore what was been said before and to concentrate on making their own point. In mixed conversation, this means that women become resentful at having their comments ignored, while men will miss the cut and thrust of conversations played according to their rules.

152

Topic shifts
Shifts between topics tend to be abrupt in all-male conversations, whereas women typically build on each others' contributions, so topics are developed progressively in conversation and topic shift occurs gradually. Elaboration and continuity are key notions in any analysis of women's talk, but are irrelevant to an understanding of men's talk.

Self-disclosure
Women tend to see conversation as an opportunity to discuss problems, share experience and offer reassurance and advice. In this respect, all-women conversations are therapeutic. For men, the discussion of personal problems is not a normal component of conversation. Men therefore respond to another speaker's disclosure as if it were a request for advice. They do not respond by bringing up their own problems, but take on the role of expert and offer advice, often lecturing the other speaker(s). The statement of a problem, then, has quite different meaning for women and men, and their linguistic responses differ accordingly.

Verbal aggressiveness
Loud and aggressive argument is a common feature of speech in all-male groups: such arguments often focus on trivial issues and are enjoyed for their own sake. Shouting, name-calling, threats and insults are all part of male verbal aggressiveness (some of these are well documented – see for example Labov (1972b) on ritual insults among black adolescents). Women, however, try to avoid displays of verbal aggressiveness – they find such displays unpleasant and interpret them as meant personally. For women, such displays represent a disruption of conversation, whereas for men they are part of the conventional structure of conversation.

Interruption
Interruptions – that is, talk by another speaker during current speaker's turn – are a normal part of relaxed informal conversation between equals. Women frequently interpolate remarks, offer enthusiastic comments, as well as nodding and making minimal responses (*mhm*, *yeah*) during another speaker's turn. In the context of all-women interaction, such behaviour is not seen as an attempt to deny the current speaker the right to complete her turn, but as evidence of active listenership. Men's interruptions, on the other hand, seem to have as their goal the seizing of a turn and therefore they *are* perceived as an attempt to deny the current speaker's right to complete a turn. In mixed conversations, as we have seen (6.2.1), men's use of interruptions results in women not talking.

Listening

In conversation, participants have two main roles, as speakers and as listeners. The evidence from all-women groups is that women value highly the role of listening. They use many minimal responses, they do not interrupt in the sense of preventing a speaker from finishing a turn (see above), and they actively encourage others to speak. Men on the other hand seem to construe conversation as a competition where the aim is to be speaker. This means that their conversational strategies involve trying to seize a turn whenever possible, and then trying to hold on to it. This results in the typical pattern in all-men groups of a few men dominating conversation while the rest say little. Listening is not highly valued by men. These two approaches to conversation inevitably lead to clashes in mixed interaction. Women's behaviour is perceived by men as a failure to assert their right to speak rather than as active listening; men's behaviour is perceived by women as insensitive to their right to speak as well as to listen (women often complain that they feel men ignore their contributions to conversation). Not surprisingly, the evidence is that in mixed interaction women speak less, initiating only about a third of all conversations.

These areas of potential miscommunication arise directly from the different overall styles of women's and men's conversations. Women tend to organise their talk **co-operatively**, while men tend to organise their talk **competitively**. These different modes of organisation entail different conversational rules. In particular, women and men differ in their expectations of what constitutes a normal component of conversation, of how conversations should progress, of how important it is to respect current speaker's right to finish a turn, and of how important it is to actively support the current speaker. In mixed-sex groups, it seems that women put far more effort than men into maintaining and facilitating conversation.

Some may view the miscommunication that arises in conversations between the sexes as an interesting clash of styles (Maltz and Borker 1982). But it can be argued that their competence in a different style disadvantages women in interaction with men. In mixed conversations, women do more of the interactive work, supporting others' topics, respecting others' turns, facilitating conversational flow through the use of questions. The end-product of all this is that men dominate conversation. This is unsatisfactory if such interactions are meant to be exchanges between equals. But is it adequate to respond that women need to change their style of talking? – many would argue that some features of women's talk are desirable for everyone. In discussions of this topic, male students have expressed to me their unhappiness at their inability to express their feelings or to discuss them with other men.[3] Both women and men, then, seem to be disadvantaged by the existence of these two different modes of conversational interaction: women because their style leads to their being dominated in mixed groups, and men because they lack competence in valuable aspects of the women's style.

9.3 LANGUAGE AND DISADVANTAGE

Chapter 6 analysed in detail certain aspects of communicative competence where male and female speakers differ. In this section we shall focus on the school – on the classroom in particular – to look at the differentiated competence of girls and boys and the way this affects their education. By analysing what goes on in the microcosm of the school setting, we shall test the claim that girls are a disadvantaged group and that the *language* girls use – and the way they use it – is in some way tied up with this disadvantage.

Disadvantage is a term widely used by those writing on education.

> 'Disadvantage . . . signifies a relatively enduring condition descriptive of the lifestyles of certain social groups – the working class, immigrant populations and ethnic minorities among them – which contributes to poor academic achievement for children at school, and generally lowered chances of success in the larger society'.
>
> (Edwards 1979b:1)

Notice that this (relatively recent) definition of disadvantage does not mention women in its examples of disadvantaged social groups. It is only recently, as we saw in Chapter 1 (1.2.1 and 1.3), that researchers have seriously considered the possibility that women are a social group in their own right, and that they are moreover a disadvantaged social group.

Educationalists tend to demonstrate a link between disadvantaged social groups and their language by looking at *dialect* differences. For example, the under-achievement of children of West Indian origin in British schools has been associated with their use of varieties of English related to creoles such as Jamaican Creole; similarly, the under-achievement of children from working-class backgrounds in British schools is often said to derive from their use of non-standard (regional) varieties of English.

No such simple link between non-standard language and disadvantage can be made for girls. To begin with, girls are members of the whole spectrum of social class and ethnic groups in society, as are boys. Female speakers are not a homogeneous group using a single dialect. Secondly, the clearest finding to emerge from the sociolinguistic studies reviewed in Chapters 4 and 5 was that female speakers tend to use more standard speech than comparable male speakers. In school, as Jenny Cheshire's (1982a) research showed, girls are more adept than boys at switching to a more standard dialect, even if their speech outside school is relatively non-standard. As far as dialect differences go, then, girls should be at an advantage rather than a disadvantage in the school setting.

Linguistically, girls in school differ from other disadvantaged groups. The significant aspect of their language use is not their pronunciation or grammar, but the wider area of their communicative competence. As we saw in Chapter 7, young children acquire language appropriate to their sex, and this includes differentiated communicative competence. In the school setting, this differing understanding of when to speak, when to remain silent, how to mark speech for politeness, when it is permissible to interrupt, etc. helps to contribute to different outcomes for girls and boys.

Their differentiated communicative competence enables boys to dominate in the classroom. Boys demand attention while girls wait patiently.

> . . . . in the jewellery class the pupils followed the teacher around asking for his advice. If there was a queue the boys would always push in in front of the girls to get the teacher's attention. One boy in particular was constantly asking the teacher's advice. (Whyte 1984:11)

Boys tend to brag; after a school test they will say it was 'easy', 'simple', while the girls tend to express anxiety about their performance (their comments are of course unrelated to their results). Boys' confidence is also apparent in the way they respond to questions: they participate actively, call out answers, make lots of guesses, while girls listen more passively (Stanworth 1981; Spender 1982; Kelly forthcoming; Kelly et al. 1984; Whyte 1984). Pupils themselves are aware of this discrepancy: 'they all make a lot of noise, all those boys. That's why I think they're more intelligent than us' (female pupil reported in Stanworth 1981:48). Girls' silence in class is despised by boys, but tends to be supported by the girls who are hostile towards girls who adopt a more assertive role. Girls are explicitly taught that loudness is 'unfeminine' (Payne 1980) and it seems that girls' sense of their own identity as female makes them feel that the speech acts of arguing, challenging and shouting are inappropriate behaviour for them.

Quietness is an ideal held up to schoolchildren throughout their school life. Many schools equate *quiet* behaviour with *nice* behaviour. The English infant school defines the quiet child as well-behaved and the noisy child as badly-behaved (King 1978:61). King asked infant teachers to rate pupils according to their conduct: the results showed that good children (in the teachers' eyes) are girls, particularly girls from the middle-class. As King comments: 'Girls seem to be closer to the definition of how children should be, than boys from the same social background' (op. cit.:126). Girls achieve this goal by conforming to the school's demand for quietness. Whether quietness *is* a desirable quality is a debatable point: recent innovations in educational practice have stressed the importance of *active* learning – for children to learn, they need to be actively involved in the learning process. Being actively involved means *talking*, among other things: asking questions, making suggestions, offering comments. The quiet child, if quiet means passive and unassertive, is a child who is unable to participate fully in learning.

One consequence of boys' more noisy, undisciplined behaviour in the classroom is that they get more attention. Recent research carried out in the United States, Britain, and Sweden, analysing teacher-pupil interaction patterns, has arrived at the same result: boys get more of the teacher's attention than girls (Sears & Feldman 1974; Spender 1982; Wernersson 1982). Spender estimates that teachers normally give two-thirds of their attention to boys.

A project known as GIST (Girls into Science and Technology) has just been completed in which a cohort of 2,000 children in ten co-educational comprehensives in Greater Manchester were followed through from the time they entered secondary school (11 years old) until they made their option choices at the end of the third year (for full details see Kelly et al. 1984). The project aimed simultaneously to explore *why* girls do not opt for science (specifically physics and chemistry) or craft subjects, *and* to initiate strategies to combat this tendency. The GIST team believed that teachers *can* change the balance of teacher-pupil interaction towards greater equality (Whyte 1984). They observed thirty-four lessons: all the teachers involved has beeen briefed on the aims of the project and all knew that girls tend to receive less attention in class. In twenty of the lessons, the teachers involved managed to give the girls as much attention as the boys or more. It should be noted that this measure was crude since it ignored the amount of talk involved (every interaction scored 1 regardless of length) and also ignored the context in which teachers addressed girls or boys. However, the GIST project does at least suggest that Spender is pessimistic in her view that teachers cannot achieve equality in their interaction with girls and boys. On the other hand, it emerged that women teachers were far more successful than men at giving girls a fair share of their attention: 75 per cent of the female teachers observed achieved an interaction ratio which was equal for girls and boys or which favoured girls, while only 50 per cent of male teachers achieved this.

Like Spender, the GIST team found that teachers' perceptions of how they interacted with pupils were at odds with quantitative observations. Most were surprised to find how much attention they gave to boys. A male head of science who successfully achieved a balance in his class remarked afterwards that 'he had *felt* as if ninety per cent of his attention was being devoted to the girls' (Whyte, 1984).

Boys normally receive both more disapproval and more praise. When girls get into trouble, it is for showing lack of knowledge or skill, whereas boys get into trouble for violating rules. By responding to boys' noisy demanding behaviour, teachers in effect reward that behaviour. Teachers' responses encourage boys to act independently, but lower girls' self-esteem. By 11 or 12, bright girls are known to have a significantly lower self-image than boys of comparable ability (Sears and Feldman, 1974).

The language pupils use to each other reflects their unequal status. Boys in secondary school often ridicule girls: they groan when girls ask questions and make rude comments. The GIST observers give examples of this, and comment that they observed *no* examples of girls ridiculing or putting down boys. The unequal roles assigned to girls and boys are well illustrated in a Dutch experiment (described in Millman 1983:7) which set out to investigate male/female interaction. Dutch children were divided into same-sex and mixed-sex pairs for a science experiment. The analysis of the resulting videos revealed that same-sex pairs worked co-operatively, but in the mixed-sex pairs the boys adopted a dominant role which the girls accepted: the boys set up the experiment and reported the results to the teacher while the girls helped and then cleared up afterwards.

Teachers' awareness of the different communicative competence of girls and boys also affects the choice of topics to be discussed in school. Lessons are organised to reflect boys' interests, because teachers have learned that boys will object – loudly – to topics they see as effeminate, while girls will accept 'boys' topics (Clarricoates 1978). Teachers have varying success in their efforts to include girls. Elizabeth Sarah (1980) involved girls in a discussion of Space Travel by using passages with the pronoun *he* changed to *she*. The boys in her class hotly disputed the idea of spacewomen, and all wrote about space*men* in the follow-up work; the girls however wrote about spacewomen. Sarah claims that they obviously felt actively involved in the class project. Elliot, on the other hand, tried to facilitate girls' participation in his lesson on the topic of War, only to find that the boys ridiculed the girls' contributions, and the girls felt very uncomfortable at being forced to assert themselves in a mixed class (Elliot, cited in Spender 1980b:150). Both these teachers have grasped the nettle of girls' non-participation in classroom discussions, but even so they have chosen as class topics subjects which are conventionally associated more with boys' interests.

In conclusion, we can say that the relationship between girls or women as a group, the language they use, and disadvantage is a complex one. First, the relationship between women and disadvantage is not always straightforward. In school, for example, girls do relatively well – this was one of the reasons why recognition of women as a disadvantaged group was slow to emerge. Girls do better than boys throughout primary school, particularly in English, and at O level/CSE girls get more passes at higher grades. However, this success rests almost entirely on girls' ability in subjects at the Humanities end of the spectrum: English, modern languages, history, etc. Four times as many boys as girls take CSE physics; three times as many boys take 0 level physics; 95 per cent of examination entries in all technical subjects are for boys (DES, 1983). This means that, despite their good results, girls are at a disadvantage in a society which values technology and science.

If we look at education outcomes in terms of what happens to pupils *after* school, it is quite clear that girls are at a disadvantage. As employees, women are concentrated in poorly paid, low prestige jobs; they constitute less than 10 per cent of those employed in the majority of top professions (architects, barristers, accountants, university professors, top civil servants, etc.). DES statistics show that 62 per cent of students in higher education (universities, polytechnics, colleges of higher education) are male.

Secondly, we have tried to show in this section that girls' use of language in school differs markedly from that of boys, and that this phenomenon is related to the relative status of girls and boys – boys use language as a means of dominating in the classroom. But saying that girls' use of language in school is related to their disadvantaged status is not the same thing as saying that girls' use of language *causes* disadvantage. Disadvantage – for any minority group – arises from the way society is organised. Girls do not fail to go on to university or to take up brilliant careers *because* of their language; they fail to do so because society dictates different (subordinate) roles for them. The fact that their disadvantage is ultimately social rather than linguistic is particularly clear in the case of female speakers. The language of ethnic minority children (whether they speak a separate language or a variety of English like London Jamaican) and the language of working-class children are clearly out of line with the language valued in school (Standard English). But this isn't true of girls: they are more successful at producing varieties closer to Standard English in the school context, and they are both polite and quiet. In other words, linguistically, girls conform to the school's norms, yet their outcomes are still poor. Clearly it is social forces, not language, that are responsible for this result.

However, this is not to deny that language may play a secondary role in disadvantaging girls. Linguistic variation is, after all, a direct reflection of social variation (see 1.4). As a minority group, girls are caught up in a process whereby social distinctions are reflected in linguistic differences which in turn *reinforce* social distinctions. A vicious circle of this kind means that, in a secondary way, language is a factor in perpetuating disadvantage. Some schools are making brave efforts to combat these social pressures, by, for example, encouraging teachers to make sure they talk to and listen to girls as much as boys, but such efforts can do little to alter the fact that society constructs male and female roles as different and *unequal*.

9.4   WOMEN, MEN AND LANGUAGE: CONCLUSIONS

This book has set out to demonstrate that in our society, and others like it, there are clear male/female differences in language. In a society where sex/gender is a highly significant category, it is not surprising that language reflects and reinforces such a category. Linguists have the task of describing and explaining the linguistic correlates of gender. The emergence of sociolinguistics as a discipline reflects the increase in studies of linguistic variation of all kinds, but while descriptions become more refined, explanations are still tentative and unsophisticated.

In this chapter we have looked at two areas where linguistic sex differences have socially undesirable consequences. In 9.2 we described ways in which women's and men's differing understanding of how conversational interaction works can lead to miscommunication. In 9.3 we looked at work in schools which suggests that, while not directly responsible for their under-achievement, the way girls use language is a contributory factor to their disadvantaged position. These two areas illustrate nicely the two different approaches to language and sex differences outlined in 1.4. Discussion of miscommunication between adult speakers in mixed conversations assumes that women and men talk differently and have different rules for conversation because they belong to different subcultures. Discussion of girls' under-achievement in the education system and its linguistic correlates, on the other hand, assumes that differences in girls' and boys' language are directly related to girls' oppression. The first approach emphasises the **difference** in the gender roles and identities of women and men, the second emphasises the hierarchical nature of gender relations and the **dominance** of men.

The two topics covered in this chapter illustrate the need for both approaches. An analysis of classroom interaction which ignored the dimension of dominance and subordination would have little explanatory power. On the other hand, to insist that the conversational patterns typical of all-women groups can be explained by calling women an oppressed group is to do them less than justice. The differences in conversational style between all-women and all-men groups are a reflection of subcultural differences: such an acknowledgement is a necessary precursor to recognising that women's talk is as deserving of sociolinguistic description in its own right as men's talk.

Language is one of the means by which individuals locate themselves in social space. Speech is an act of identity: when we speak, one of the things we do is identify ourselves as male or female. During childhood and adolescence we learn linguistic behaviour appropriate to our sex, and this becomes part of our identity. The reason we need a two-pronged approach to linguistic sex differences results from a simple fact: since there are two sexes, conversations can either be same-sex or mixed-sex. These contexts are significantly different: when all participants in a conversation are the same sex, then the existence of a gender hierarchy is irrelevant; when participants are of both sexes, then dominance and oppression become relevant categories. This fact is particularly relevant to women and their language – when they interact with men they are relating to superiors (all other things being equal), but when they interact with other women they interact as equals. So we need both approaches to deal with the complexities of language differences between women and men.

It is important to note that, until very recently, research involving linguistic sex differences was conducted by *men* (see also the section on dialectologists, 3.5.3). This means that male informants were being asked to talk to another man, while female informants were being asked to talk in a mixed-sex context. It will be some time before we are sure that findings such as women's use of more polite forms and their use of linguistic variants closer to Standard English are not an artefact of the research situation.

There is a great deal still to be done in the area of sex differences and language. There is a need for more detailed sociolinguistic studies at both individual and group levels. We must remember that sex differentiation in language does not exist in a vacuum – it interacts in a complex way with other kinds of social differentiation. More crucially, there is a need for a more sophisticated theory of society: without this we cannot begin to understand or explain the processes which cause and maintain linguistic differences. Sex/gender is an important category in all known societies: linguistic variation correlating with this social distinction is presumably a universal feature of speech communities. In this book I have aimed to summarise what is known about the co-variation of language and sex. It is hoped that this will lead to a better understanding of women's language use and men's language use, and of the linguistic relationship between the sexes.

NOTES

1 Many of the generalisations in this section refer more accurately to white middle-class women and to white middle-class men – however, Goodwin's work on the language of black children in Philadelphia (Goodwin 1980) and Wodak's work on the language of working-class adults in Vienna (Wodak 1981) confirm the general pattern. (Goodwin's work is discussed in 6.2.2; Wodak's work is discussed in 6.5.) Research by Bent Preisler (described briefly on p. 117n1), which looked at women and men in three occupational groups (managerial, clerical, and manual) in both mixed- and single-sex groups, shows that many linguistic features are typical of women's speech regardless of age or social class.

2 This summary draws on the work of Aries 1976; Jones 1980; Kalcik 1975; Wodak 1981.

3 Teachers at Hackney Downs Boys School in London found that 'boys' ways of communicating with each other within the classroom tended to be rigid, stylised, and competitive, often making it impossible to discuss issues in a personal or meaningful way' (*Guardian* Women, 12 March 1985). They have therefore started a Skills for Living course aimed, among other things, at helping the boys to talk about themselves.

Select Bibliography

Argyle, M., Lalljee, M. and **Cook, M.** (1968) The effects of visibility on interaction in a dyad, *Human Relations*, 21, 3–17.
Aries, E. (1976) Interaction patterns and themes of male, female and mixed groups, *Small Group Behaviour*, vol. 7 no. 1., 7–18.
Bem, S. (1974) The measurement of psychological androgyny, *Journal of Consulting and Clinical Psychology*, 42, 155–62.
Bem, S. (1975) Sex role adaptability: one consequence of psychological androgyny, *Journal of Personality and Social Psychology*, 31 no. 4, 634–43.
Bernard, J. (1972) *The Sex Game*. Atheneum, New York.
Blom, J. P. and **Gumperz, J.** (1972) Social meaning in linguistic structures: code switching in Norway, pp 407–34 in Gumperz, J. and Hymes, D. (eds) *Directions in Sociolinguistics*. Holt Rinehart & Winston, New York.
Bloom, L. (1970) *Language Development: Form and Function in Emerging Grammars*. M.I.T. Press, Cambridge, Massachusetts.
Bloom, L. (1975) *One Word At A Time*. Mouton, The Hague.
Bloomfield, L. (1933) *Language*. George Allen & Unwin, London.
Bodine, A. (1975a) Sex differentiation in language, pp 130–51 in Thorne, B. and Henley, N. (eds) *Language and Sex: Difference and Dominance*. Newbury House Publishers, Rowley, Massachusetts.
Bodine, A. (1975b) Androcentrism in prescriptive grammar, *Language in Society*, vol. 4 no. 2, 129–56.
Bosmajian, H. (1974) *The Language of Oppression*. Public Affairs Press, Washington D.C.
Bragg, M. and **Ellis, S.** (1976) Word of Mouth. BBC TV, London.
Breakwell, G. (1979) Women: group and identity?, *Women's Studies International Quarterly*, 2, 9–17.
Bridge, J. C. (1917) *Cheshire Proverbs and Other Sayings and* ·

Rhymes Connected with the City and County Palatine of Chester.
Phillipson and Golder, Chester.

Brouwer, D., Gerritsen, M. and **Dettaan, D.** (1979) Speech
differences between women and men: on the wrong track?,
Language in Society, **8**, 33–50.

Brown, P. (1980) How and why are women more polite: some
evidence from a Mayan community, pp 111–36 in
McConnell-Ginet, S. et al. (eds). *Women and Language in
Literature and Society*. Praeger, New York.

Brown, P. and **Levinson, S.** (1978) Universals in language usage:
politeness phenomena, pp 56–289 in Goody, E. (ed.) *Questions
and Politeness*. Cambridge University Press.

Brown, R. (1976) *A First Language*. Penguin Books,
Harmondsworth.

Brun A. (1946) *Parlers régionaux, France dialectale et unité
française*. Didier, Paris.

Bruner, E. M. and **Kelso, J. P.** (1980) Gender differences in
graffiti: a semiotic perspective, in Kramarae, C. (ed.) *The
Voices and Words of Women and Men*. Pergamon Press,
Oxford.

Cameron, D. (1985) *Feminism and Linguistic Theory*. Macmillan,
London.

Cameron, D. and **Coates, J.** (1985) Some problems in the
sociolinguistic explanation of sex differences, *Language and
Communication*, vol. 5. no. 3, 143–151.

Chaney, J. (1981) *Social Networks and job information – the
situation of women who return to work*. EOC/SSRC,
Manchester.

Cheshire, J. (1978) Present tense verbs in reading English,
pp 52–68 in Trudgill, P. (ed.) *Sociolinguistic Patterns in British
English*. Edward Arnold, London.

Cheshire, J. (1982a) *Variation in an English Dialect*. Cambridge
University Press.

Cheshire, J. (1982b) Linguistic variation and social function,
pp 153–66 in Romaine S. (ed.) *Sociolinguistic Variation in
Speech Communities*. Edward Arnold, London.

Cheshire, J. (1984) Language and sexism, in Trudgill, P. (ed.)
Applications of Sociolinguistics. Academic Press, London.

Clarke-Stewart, A. (1973) Interactions between mothers and their
young children: characteristics and consequences, *Monographs
of the Society for Research in Child Development*, **153**
vol. 38 nos 6–7.

Clarricoates, K. (1978) 'Dinosaurs in the classroom': A
re-examination of some aspects of the 'hidden' curriculum in
primary schools, *Women's Studies International Quarterly*,
vol. 1 no. 4, 353–64.

Coates, J. (1984a) Syntactic variation on Merseyside, Paper presented to the SSRC workshop on varieties of British English syntax, University of Salford, January 8–10.

Coates, J. (1984b) *Language and Sexism*, CLIE Working Paper no. 4.

Crystal, D. and **Davy, D.** (1975) *Advanced Conversational English*. Longman, London.

Dale, P. (1976) *Language Development*. Holt Rinehart & Winston, New York (2nd edn).

Davies, R. T. (ed.) (1963) *Medieval English Lyrics*. Faber & Faber, London.

De Lyon, H. (1981) A sociolinguistic study of aspects of the Liverpool accent. Unpublished M. Phil. thesis, University of Liverpool.

Deuchar, M. (forthcoming) Sociolinguistics, in Lyons, J. (ed.) *New Horizons in Linguistics 2*. Penguin Books, Harmondsworth.

Deuchar, M. and **Martin-Jones, M.** (1982) Linguistic research in minority and majority communities: goals and methods. Paper given at the Sociolinguistics Symposium, Sheffield, March 29–31 1982.

Dobson, E. J. (1969) Early modern standard English, in Lass, R. (ed.) *Approaches to English Historical Linguistics*. Holt Rinehart & Winston, New York.

Dubois, B. L. and **Crouch, I.** (1975) The question of tag questions in women's speech: they don't really use more of them, do they?, *Language in Society*, **4**, 289–94.

Eakins, B. W. and **Eakins, R. G.** (1978) *Sex Differences in Human Communication*. Houghton Mifflin Company, Boston.

Edelsky, C. (1976) The acquisition of communicative competence: recognition of linguistic correlates of sex roles, *Merril-Palmer Quarterly*, **22**, 47–59.

Edelsky, C. (1977) Acquisition of an aspect of communicative competence: learning what it means to talk like a lady, in Ervin-Tripp, S. and Mitchell-Kernan, C. (eds) *Child Discourse*. Academic Press, New York.

Edwards, J. R. (1979a) Social class differences and the identification of sex in children's speech, *Journal of Child Language*, **6**, 121–27.

Edwards, J. R. (1979b) *Language and Disadvantage*. Edward Arnold, London.

Edwards, V. K. (1979) *The West Indian Language Issue in British Schools*. Routledge & Kegan Paul, London.

Ellis, H. (1894) *Man and Woman*, Walter Scott Publishing Co., London.

Elyan, O., Smith, P., Giles, H. and **Bourhis, R.** (1978)

RP-accented female speech: the voice of perceived androgyny?, pp 122–31 in Trudgill, P. (ed.) *Sociolinguistic Patterns in British English*. Edward Arnold, London.

Elyot, T. (1531) *The Governour*. The Scolar Press Ltd, Menston, Yorks, 1970.

Engle, M. (1980a) Family influences on the language development of young children, pp 259–66 in Kramarae, C. (ed.) *The Voices and Words of Women and Men*. Pergamon Press, Oxford.

Engle, M. (1980b) Language and play: a comparative analysis of parental initiatives, in Giles, Robinson and Smith (eds) *Language: social psychological perspectives*. Pergamon Press, Oxford.

Ervin-Tripp, S. (1972) An analysis of the interaction of language, topic and listener, in Fishman, J. (ed.) *Readings in the Sociology of Language*. Mouton, The Hague.

Fichtelius, A., Johansson, I. and Nordin, K. (1980) Three investigations of sex-associated speech variation in day school, pp 219–25 in Kramarae, C. (ed.) *The Voices and Words of Women and Men*. Pergamon Press, Oxford.

Fischer, J. L. (1964) Social influences on the choice of a linguistic variant, in Hymes, D. (ed.) *Language in Culture and Society*. Harper International, New York.

Fishman, P. (1978) Interaction: the work women do, *Social Problems*, **24**, 397–406.

Fishman, P. (1980) Conversational insecurity, pp. 127–32 in Giles, Robinson and Smith (eds) *Language: social psychological perspectives*. Pergamon Press, Oxford.

Flannery, R. (1946) Men's and women's speech in Gros Ventre, *International Journal of American Linguistics*, **12**, 133–5.

Flexner, S. B. (1960) Preface to *Dictionary of American Slang*. Thomas Y. Crowell, New York.

Francis, W. N. (1983) *Dialectology: an introduction*. Longman, London.

Frazer, J. G. (1900) A suggestion as to the origin of gender in language, *Fortnightly Review*, **73**, 79–90.

Gardette, P. (1968) *Atlas linguistique et ethnographique du Lyonnais*, volume IV: Expose methodologique et tables. Centre Nationale de la Recherche scientifique, Paris.

Gauchat, L. (1905) *L'unite phonetique dans le patois d'une commune*. D. S. Niemeyer, Halle.

Giles, H., Robinson, W. P. and Smith P. M. (eds) *Language: Social Psychological Perspectives*. Pergamon Press, Oxford.

Gleason, J. B. (1980) The acquisition of social speech routines and politeness formulas, in Giles, Robinson and Smith (eds).

Gomm, I. (1981) A study of the inferior image of the female use of the English language as compared to that of the male.

Unpublished B. A. dissertation, Edge Hill College, Ormskirk.
Goodwin, M. H. (1980) Directive-response speech sequences in girls' and boys' task activities, pp 157–73 in McConnell-Ginet et al. (eds) *Women and Language in Literature and Society*. Praeger, New York.
Goody, E. (ed.) (1978) *Questions and Politeness*. Cambridge University Press.
Grant, W. (1914) *The Pronunciation of English in Scotland*. Cambridge University Press.
Greif, E. B. (1980) Sex differences in parent-child conversations, pp 253–8 in Kramarae, C. (ed.) *The Voices and Words of Women and Men*. Pergamon Press, Oxford.
Gumperz, J. (ed.) *Language and Social Identity*. Cambridge University Press.
Haas, M. (1944) Men's and women's speech in Koasati, *Language*, **20**, 147–9.
Haas, A. (1978) Sex-associated features of spoken language by four-, eight-, and twelve-year-old boys and girls. Paper given at the 9th World Congress of Sociology, Uppsala, Sweden, August 14–19.
Haas, A. (1979) Male and female spoken language differences: stereotypes and evidence, *Psychological Bulletin*, **86**, 616–26.
Hirschmann, L. (1974) Analysis of supportive and assertive behaviour in conversations. Paper presented at Linguistic Society of America meeting, July 1974.
Holland, J. (1980) *Work and Women*, Bedford Way Papers 6. University of London Institute of Education.
Holmes, J. (1984) Hedging your bets and sitting on the fence: some evidence for hedges as support structures, *Te Reo*, **27**, 47–62.
Humphrey, C. (1978) Women, taboo and the suppression of attention, pp 89–108 in Ardener, S. (ed.) *Defining Females: the nature of women in society*. Croom Helm, London.
Hymes, D. (ed.) (1964) *Language in Culture and Society*. Harper International, New York.
Hymes, D. (1972) On communicative competence, pp 269–93 in Pride, J. B. and Holmes, J. (eds.) *Sociolinguistics*. Penguin Books, Harmondsworth.
Jespersen, O. (1922) *Language, Its Nature Development and Origin*. George Allen & Unwin Ltd, London.
Jones, D. (1980) Gossip: notes on women's oral culture, pp 193–8 in Kramarae, C. (ed.) *The Voices and Words of Women and Men*. Pergamon Press, Oxford.
Kalcik, S. (1975) '. . . like Ann's gynaecologist or the time I was almost raped' – personal narratives in women's rap groups, *Journal of American Folklore*, **88**, 3–11.

167

Kamuf, P. (1980) Writing like a woman, pp 284–99 in
McConnell-Ginet et al. (eds) *Women and Language in
Literature and Society*. Praeger, New York.

Kelly, A. (forthcoming) The construction of masculine science,
British Journal of the Sociology of Education

Kelly, A., Whyte, J. and Smail, B. (1984) *Girls Into Science and
Technology: Final Report*. Equal Opportunities Commission,
Manchester.

Kessler, S. and McKenna, W. (1978) *Gender: an ethno-
methodological approach*. John Wiley & Sons, New York.

Key, M. R. (1975) *Male/female Language*. Scarecrow Press,
Metuchen, New Jersey.

King, R. (1978) *All Things Bright and Beautiful?* John Wiley &
Sons, New York.

Kirkby, J. (1746) *A New English Grammar*. The Scolar Press
Ltd, Menston, Yorks, 1971.

Knowles, G. (1974) *Scouse: the urban dialect of Liverpool*.
Unpublished Ph. D. thesis, University of Leeds.

Kramer, C. (1974) Folklinguistics, *Psychology Today*, 8, 82–5.

Kramer, C. (1975) Stereotypes of women's speech: the word from
cartoons, *Journal of Popular Culture*, vol. 8 part 3, 624–38.

Kramarae, C. (ed.) (1980a) *The Voices and Words of Women and
Men*. Pergamon Press, Oxford.

Kramarae, C. (1980b) Perceptions and politics in language and sex
research, in Giles, Robinson & Smith (eds) *Language: Social
Psychological Perspectives*. Pergamon Press, Oxford.

Kramarae, C. (1981) *Women and Men Speaking*. Newbury House,
Rowley, Massachusetts.

Kramarae, C. (1982) Gender: How she speaks, in Ryan & Giles
(eds) *Attitudes Towards Language Variation*. Edward Arnold,
London.

Kurath, H. (1972) *Studies in Area Linguistics*. Indiana University
Press.

Labov, W. (1969) The logic of non-standard English, *Georgetown
Monographs on Language and Linguistics*, 22, 1–31.

Labov, W. (1971) Variation in Language, in Reed, C. E. (ed.) *The
Learning of Language*. National Council of Teachers of English,
New York.

Labov, W. (1972a) *Sociolinguistic Patterns*. University of
Pennsylvania Press, Philadelphia.

Labov, W. (1972b) *Language in the Inner City*. University of
Pennsylvania Press, Philadelphia.

Lakoff, R. (1975) *Language and Woman's Place*. Harper & Row,
New York.

Leet-Pellegrini, H. M. (1980) Conversational dominance as a
function of gender and expertise, pp 97–104 in Giles, Robinson

and Smith (eds) *Language: Social Psychological Perspectives*. Pergamon Press, Oxford.

Liebermann, P. (1967) *Intonation, Perception and Language*. M.I.T. Press, Cambridge.

Local, J. (1982) Modelling intonational variability in children's speech, pp 85–103 in Romaine, S. (ed.) *Sociolinguistic Variation in Speech Communities*. Edward Arnold, London.

Macaulay, R. K. S. (1977) *Language, Social Class and Education*. Edinburgh University Press.

Macaulay, R. K. S. (1978) Variation and consistency in Glaswegian English, pp 132–43 in Trudgill, P. (ed.) *Sociolinguistic Patterns in British English*. Edward Arnold, London.

Maccoby, E. E. and **Jacklin, C. N.** (1974) *The Psychology of Sex Differences*. Stanford University Press, Stanford.

McConnell-Ginet, S., Borker, R. and **Furman, N.** (eds) *Women and Language in Literature and Society*. Praeger, New York.

MacDonald, M. (1980) Schooling and the reproduction of class and gender relations, in Barton L., Meighan R. and Walkers S. (eds) *Schooling, Ideology and the Curriculum*. The Falmer Press.

McIntosh, A. (1952) *An Introduction to a Survey of Scottish Dialects*. Nelson.

MacLean, I. (1980) The Renaissance Notion of Woman. Cambridge University Press.

Maltz D. N. and **Borker, R. A.** (1982) A cultural approach to male-female miscommunication, pp 195–216 in Gumperz, J. (ed.) *Language and Social Identity*. Cambridge University Press.

Meditch, A. (1975) The development of sex-specific patterns in young children, *Anthropological Linguistics*, vol. 17 no. 9, 421–33.

Millman, V. (1983) *Sex Stereotyping in Schools: the role and responsibilities of the teacher*. Equal Opportunities Commission, Manchester.

Milroy, J. and **Milroy L.** (1978) Belfast: change and variation in an urban vernacular, pp 19–36 in Trudgill, P. (ed.) *Sociolinguistic Patterns in British English*. Edward Arnold, London.

Milroy, J. and **Milroy L.** (1985) Linguistic change, social network and speaker innovation, *Journal of Linguistics*, **21**, 339–84.

Milroy, L. (1980) *Language and Social Networks*. Basil Blackwell, Oxford.

Milroy, L. (1982) Social network and linguistic focusing, pp 141–52 in Romaine S. (ed.) *Sociolinguistic Variation in Speech Communities*. Edward Arnold, London.

Montaiglon, A. and **Raynaud, G.** (eds) (1872–90) *Recuil general et complet des fabliaux des XIIIe et XIVe siecles* (6 vols). Librairie des Bibliophiles, Paris.

Muscatine, C. (1981) Courtly literature and vulgar language, in Burgess, G. S. (ed.) *Court and Poet, Selected Proceedings of the 3rd Congress of the ICLS (Liverpool 1980)*, Liverpool.

Nelson, K. (1973) Structure and strategy in learning to talk, *Monographs of the Society for Research in Child Development*, no. 149, vol. **38**, no. 1–2.

Newbrook, M. (1982) Sociolinguistic reflexes of dialect interference in West Wirral. Unpublished Ph. D. thesis, Reading University.

O'Barr, W. and **Atkins, B.** (1980) 'Women's language' or 'powerless language'?, pp 93–110 in McConnell-Ginet et al. (eds) *Women and Language in Literature and Society*. Praeger, New York.

Ochs, E. and **Schieffelin, B.** (1983) *Acquiring Conversational Competence*. Routledge & Kegan Paul, London.

Orton, H. (1962) *Introduction to the Survey of English Dialects*. E. J. Arnold, Leeds.

Patterson, D. (1860) *The Provincialisms of Belfast Pointed Out and Corrected*. Belfast.

Payne, I. (1980) A working-class girl in a grammar school, pp 12–19 in Spender, D. and Sarah, E. (eds) *Learning to Lose*. The Women's Press, London.

Pee, W. (1946) *Dialect-Atlas van West-Vlaanderen en Fransch-Vlaanderen*. De Sikkel, Antwerp.

Perkins, M. (1983) *Modal Expressions in English*. Frances Pinter, London.

Poole, J. (1646) *The English Accidence*. The Scolar Press Ltd, Menston, Yorks, 1967.

Pop, S. (1950) *La Dialectologie: Apercu historique et methodes d'enquetes linguistiques*. Université de Louvain.

Preisler, B. (unpublished) *Linguistic Sex Roles in Conversation: Social Variation in the Expression of Tentativeness in English*.

Reid, E. (1976) Social and stylistic variation in the speech of some Edinburgh schoolchildren. Unpublished M. Litt. thesis, University of Edinburgh.

Reid, E. (1978) Social and stylistic variation in the speech of children: some evidence from Edinburgh, pp 158–71 in Trudgill, P. (ed.) *Sociolinguistic Patterns in British English*. Arnold, London.

Romaine, S. (1978) Postvocalic /r/ in Scottish English: sound change in progress?, pp 144–57 in Trudgill, P. (ed.) *Sociolinguistic Patterns in British English*. Edward Arnold, London.

Romaine, S. (ed.) (1982) *Sociolinguistic Variation in Speech Communities*. Edward Arnold, London.

Romaine, S. (1984) *The Language of Children and Adolescents: The Acquisition of communicative competence*. Basil Blackwell, Oxford.

Rosaldo, M. Z. and **Lamphere, L.** (eds) (1974) *Woman, Culture and Society*. Stanford University Press.

Ryan, E. B. and **Giles, H.** (eds) (1982) *Attitudes Towards Language Variation*. Edward Arnold, London.

Sachs, J., Lieberman, P. and **Erickson, D.** (1973) Anatomical and cultural determinants of male and female speech, pp 74–84 in Shuy, R. and Fasold, R. (eds) *Language Attitudes: current trends and prospects*. Georgetown University Press, Washington.

Sacks, H., Schegloff, E. A. and **Jefferson, G.** (1974) A simplest systematics for the organisation of turn-taking for conversation, *Language, 50*, 696–735.

Sapir, E. (1961) Male and female forms of speech in Yana, in Mandelbaum, D. (ed.) *Selected Writings of Edward Sapir on Language, Culture and Personality*. University of California Press, Berkeley.

Sarah, E. (1980) Teachers and students in the classroom: an examination of classroom interaction, pp 155–64 in Spender, D. and Sarah, E. (eds) *Learning to Lose*. The Women's Press, London.

Sears, P. and **Feldman, D.** (1974) Teacher interactions with boys and with girls, in Stacey, J., Bereaud, S. and Daniels, J. (eds) *And Jill Came Tumbling After: sexism in American education*. Dell Publishing, New York.

Shipman, V. C. (1971) Disadvantaged children and their first school experiences, Educational Testing Service Head Start Longitudinal Study.

Siegler, D. and **Siegler, R.** (1976) Stereotypes of males' and females' speech, *Psychological Reports, 39*, 167–70.

Smith, P. M. (1979) Sex markers in speech, pp 109–46 in Scherer, K. R. and Giles, H. (eds) *Social Markers in Speech*. Cambridge University Press.

Smith R. K. and **Connolly K.** (1972) Patterns of play and social interaction in pre-school children, in Jones N. B. (ed.) *Ethological Studies of Child Behaviour*. Cambridge University Press.

Smith, W. G. and **Heseltine, J. E.** (eds) (1935) *The Oxford Dictionary of English Proverbs*. Oxford University Press.

Soskin, W. and **John, V.** (1963) The study of spontaneous talk, in Barker, R. (ed.) *The Stream of Behaviour*. Appleton-Century-Crofts, New York.

171

Spender, D. (1980a) *Man Made Language*. Routledge & Kegan Paul, London.

Spender, D. (1980b) Talking in class, pp 148–54 in Spender, D. and Sarah E. (eds) *Learning to Lose*. The Women's Press, London.

Spender, D. (1982) *Invisible Women – The Schooling Scandal*. Writers and Readers Publishing Cooperative, London.

Spender, D. and **Sarah, E.** (eds) (1980) *Learning to Lose*. The Women's Press, London.

Stanford Research Institute (1972) Follow-through pupil tests, parent interviews, and teacher questionnaires, Appendix C.

Stanworth, M. (1981) *Gender and Schooling*. WRRC Publications Collective.

Stone, M. (1983) Learning to say it in cup of tea language, *The Guardian* (Women's Page), 19 April 1983.

Strodtbeck, F. and **Mann, R.** (1956) Sex role differentiation in jury deliberations, *Sociometry*, **19**, 3–11.

Swacker, M. (1975) The sex of the speaker as a sociolinguistic variable, pp. 76–83 in Thorne, B. and Henley, N. (eds) *Language and Sex*. Newbury House, Rowley, Massachusetts.

Swift, J. (1735) *Works*. Faulkner, Dublin.

Tajfel, H. (1974) Social identity and intergroup behaviour, *Social Science Information*, **13**(2), 65–93.

Tajfel, H. (ed.) (1978) *Differentiation Between Social Groups: studies in the social psychology of intergroup relations*. Academic Press, London.

Tajfel, H. (1981) *Human Groups and Social Categories*. Cambridge University Press.

Thorne, B. and **Henley, N.** (eds) *Language and Sex: difference and dominance*. Newbury House, Rowley, Massachusetts.

Trudgill, P. (1972) Sex, covert prestige and linguistic change in the urban British English of Norwich, *Language in Society*, **1**, 179–95.

Trudgill, P. (1974a) *The Social Differentiation of English in Norwich*. Cambridge University Press.

Trudgill, P. (1974b) *Sociolinguistics*. Penguin Books, Harmondsworth.

Trudgill, P. (ed.) (1978) *Sociolinguistic Patterns in British English*. Edward Arnold, London.

Trudgill, P. (1983) *On Dialect*. Basil Blackwell, Oxford.

Trudgill, P. (1984) *Applications of Sociolinguistics*. Academic Press, London.

Tucker, S. (1961) *English Examined*. Cambridge University Press.

Walters, J. (1981) Variation in the requesting behaviour of bilingual children, *International Journal of the Sociology of Language*, **27**, 77–92.

Weitz, S. (1977) *Sex Roles: biological, psychological and social foundations*. Oxford University Press.

Wells, G. (1979) Variation in child language, in Lee, V. (ed.) *Language Development*. Croom Helm, London.

Wernersson, I. (1982) Sex differentiation and teacher-pupil interaction in Swedish compulsory schools, in Secretariat of the Council of Europe (ed.) *Sex Stereotyping in Schools*. Swets and Zeitlinger.

Whyte, J. (1984) Observing sex stereotypes and interactions in the school lab and workshop, *Educational Review*, **36**, 75–86.

Williams, I. F. (1912) *Phonetics for Scottish Students: the sounds of polite Scottish described and compared with those of polite English* (2nd edn). James Maclehose & Sons, Glasgow.

Williams, J. and **Giles, H.** (1978) The changing status of women in society: an intergroup perspective, pp 431–46 in Tajfel, H. (ed.) *Differentiation Between Social Groups*. Academic Press, London.

Wilson, T. (1560) *The Arte of Rhetorique*. Clarendon Press, London (1909).

Wilson, T. (1724) *The Many Advantages of a Good Language to Any Nation*. The Scolar Press Ltd, Menston, Yorks, 1969.

Wodak, R. (1981) Women relate, men report: sex differences in language behaviour in a therapeutic group, *Journal of Pragmatics*, **5**, 261–85.

Woolf, V. (1979) *Women and Writing*. The Women's Press, London.

Yaguello, M. (1978) *Les mots et les femmes*. Petite Bibliothèque Payot, Paris.

Zimin, S. (1981) Sex and politeness: factors in first- and second-language use, *International Journal of the Sociology of Language*, **27**, 35–58.

Zimmerman, D. and **West, C.** (1975) Sex roles, interruptions and silences in conversation, pp 105–29 in Thorne, B. and Henley, N. (eds) *Language and Sex: difference and dominance*. Newbury House, Rowley, Massachusetts.

Index

175

176

O'Barr, W., 112–14, 117 n1
oppression, 12, 160–2
over-report, 72–3

parataxis, 25–6
participant observation, 5, 81, 85
peer group, 85, 87, 88, 94, 149
    pressure, 92, 94
    status, 87
Perkins, M., 123, 130
phonological
    differences, 35–6, 63–71 *passim*
    variation *see* variation,
        phonological
phonology, 47, 96, 121, 140
politeness, 109–12, 117, 129, 130–1,
    133, 160, 161
power, 101, 115
powerful language, 112–14
powerless language, 112–14, 117
prestige, 57, 74, 75
    form/variant, 59, 60, 62, 63, 66,
        68–71 *passim*, 72, 73, 74
    see also norm, prestige
pronunciation, 29–31, 35–6, 43, 96,
    136, 139, 142, 156
psychological androgyny *see* androgyny

quantitative sociolinguistic studies, 13,
    30, 51, 57–78 *passim*, 138–50
    passim
questionnaire, 46–9
questions, 105–6, 117
    meaning of, 152
quiet behaviour, 33, 156–7, 160
    see also silence

Reading, 85–91 *passim*
role *see* sex role
Romaine, S., 69–71, 127–9, 139,
    141–2
R.P., 29, 72, 75–6, 142, 144, 148
    speakers, 75–7

school, 33, 92, 151, 155–60, 161
Scouse, 67, 72
self-evaluation tests, 72–3
sensitivity
    of lower middle class, 63
    of women, 43, 71–2, 73, 112, 149
sex, 4, 5, 8, 51, 58, 63, 160, 162
sex-appropriate behaviour *see*
    appropriate
sex-exclusive differences, 40, 132
sex-preferential differences, 40, 132,
    134
sex role, 40, 133, 149, 158–61
sexism, 3
    sexist, 26, 28, 45, 122
silence, 33–4, 100, 103, 116, 156
social class, 4, 5, 8, 34 n2, 51, 57, 58,
    68, 74, 77, 123, 155, 162 n1
social group, 4, 76, 122, 136, 155–60
    passim
    women as, 7–12

social network, 13, 79–95, 147, 149
    density, 80
    multiplexity, 80
social psychology, 3, 8, 75–6
social stratification, 57, 58–61, 142,
    143, 144
social variation *see* variation
sociolinguistics, 3, 4–7, 40–1, 51, 95,
    138, 160
    see also quantitative sociolinguistic
        studies
solidarity, 75–7, 92, 102, 115, 117, 140,
    149
speaker innovation *see* innovation
speech community, 5, 40, 51, 91, 117
    homogeneous, 5, 40
Spender, D., 34, 103, 156, 157, 158,
    159
stable linguistic variable *see* linguistic
    variable
standardisation, 57
Standard English, 5, 16, 22, 40, 73, 74,
    78, 91, 92–3, 125, 149, 159, 161
status, 75–7, 114, 149, 158, 159
    status-based model, 92
    status-consciousness, 43
stigma, 57
    stigmatised form, 29, 63, 65, 71, 72,
        73, 128
stratification *see* social stratification
style-shifting, 65, 92, 129, 139, 148
stylistic variation *see* variation
subculture, 12, 160
subordination *see* oppression
support, 102, 115, 117
Survey of English Dialects, 43, 45
swearing, 19–22, 108–9, 117, 131, 133
syntax, 96
    syntactic features, 86

taboo, 38–9
    language, 19–22, 108–9, 133
tag questions, 103–5, 118 n2, 131
Tajfel, H., 8–12
talkativeness *see* verbosity
topic, 103, 129, 131, 151–2, 158–9
    topic-control, 101–2, 116
    topic-shift, 153
Trudgill, P., 57, 59–61, 63–6, 72–3,
    78 n2, 139, 142–5
turn-taking in conversation, 97–102,
    152
Tyneside, 125–7

under-report, 73

variable *see* linguistic variable
variation, 3, 22
    linguistic, 4, 12, 40, 41, 51, 57, 63,
        77, 136, 150, 160, 161–2
    phonological, 127–9
    social, 4, 61, 136, 150, 160, 161–2
    stylistic, 4, 61, 136, 140
verbosity, 31–4, 103, 129, 133